POETRY RE

SPRING 1999 VOLUME
CO-EDITORS PETER FORBES J
PRODUCTION STEPHEN T
ADVERTISING LISA ROBERTS

CONTENTS

All illustrations by Gerald Mangan

LONDON MAGAZINE

FICTION * MEMOIRS * CRITICISM * POETRY

CINEMA * ARCHITECTURE * PHOTOGRAPHY

THEATRE * ART * MUSIC

'A fantastic magazine whose place in the history of 20th century literary life grows ever more secure and significant' – *William Boyd, Evening Standard*
Each issue contains over 50 pages of poems and reviews of poetry.

NEW LME POETRY

Herbert Lomas *A Hopeless Passion*

Ted Walker *Mangoes on the Moon*

Robert Conquest *Demons Don't*

Nikos Kavvadias *Wireless Operator*

To be published in May, £7.95 each

Soon in London Magazine
Tom Pickard on the life of Basil Bunting
features on Ewart Milne, Hugo Manning, C. H. Sisson

Subscriptions:
£28.50 p.a. (six issues) to 30 Thurloe Place, London SW7

Single copies £5.99 from discriminating bookshops

POETRY REVIEW
SUBSCRIPTIONS
Four issues including postage:

UK individuals £27
Overseas individuals £35
(all overseas delivery is by airmail)
USA individuals $56

Libraries, schools and institutions:
UK £35
Overseas £42
USA $66

Single issue £6.95 + 50p p&p (UK)

Sterling and US dollar payments only.
Eurocheques, Visa and Mastercard
payments are acceptable.

Bookshop distribution:
Signature
Telephone 0161 834 8767

Design by Philip Lewis
Cover by Stephen Troussé

Typeset by Poetry Review.

Printed by Grillford Ltd at
26 Peverel Drive, Bletchley,
Milton Keynes MK1 1QZ
Telephone: 01908 644123

POETRY REVIEW is the magazine of the
Poetry Society. It is published quarterly
and issued free to members of the Poetry
Society. Poetry Review considers submis-
sions from non-members and members
alike. To ensure reply submissions must
be accompanied by an SAE or adequate
International Reply coupons: Poetry
Review accepts no responsibility for
contributions that are not reply paid.

Founded 24 February 1909
Charity Commissioners No: 303334
© 1999

POETRY SOCIETY

THE POETRY SOCIETY

EDITORIAL AND BUSINESS ADDRESS:
22 BETTERTON STREET, LONDON WC2H 9BU

telephone **0171 420 9880**
fax **0171 240 4818**
email **poetrysoc@dial.pipex.com**
website **http://www.poetrysoc.com**

Australia Council
for the Arts

ISBN 1 900771 13 6
ISSN 0032 2156

Funded by
THE
ARTS
COUNCIL
OF ENGLAND

THE REPUBLIC OF SPRAWL

BY PETER FORBES

IT IS USEFUL to be timely in any activity, and Australia's time seems to have come, thanks in no small part to my co-editor on this issue, John Kinsella. There have been several anthologies published in the UK in recent years and two new ones, as yet only available in Australia, are considered in this issue. Kinsella's new anthology *Landbridge** is perhaps the best State-of-the-Art guide available. Many of the poets included are also in this issue of *Poetry Review*.

We hope that this issue will provide a useful starting point for readers yet to see past the commanding figure of Les Murray and that within Australia it should provide a snapshot of the current scene. As the English editor, I particularly enjoyed choosing poems from the harvest gathered by John Kinsella. The results are refreshingly different from the usual crop.

Although John Kinsella dissociates himself from the schism that exists in Australian poetry between the traditionalists led by Les Murray and the experimentalists under John Tranter – he is equally at home with both camps – English readers will need to know about it to get their bearings. It is of course a similar divide to that which exists in English and American poetry but it is certainly deeper-rooted than it is here. The reason is that the experimental school is far more powerful and central than it is in Britain. One of the driving forces of the Ern Malley Affair was Australia's powerful need in the '30s to throw off its outback image and to embrace international modernism. This was a far more compelling need than it was in the old culture of England.

The ferocity of the battle in recent times owes something to the extraordinary phenomenon of that same Les Murray. It is impossible for anyone, inside or outside Australia, to take their bearings without considering him. Les Murray's work became unignorable in England because you didn't have to be Australian to appreciate the original sensibility behind 'The Quality of Sprawl' and 'The Dream of Wearing Shorts Forever'. Perhaps we misread him somewhat because we can take the life-enhancing generosity of these poems and leave behind the more parochial struggles he is sometimes involved in. I have always thought English readers should reflect hard on his lines "Some of us primary producers, us farmers and authors / are going to watch them evict a banker". A country in which farmers are now complaining that, besides being ruined financially by falling livestock prices, they have been totally marginalized by postmodern city culture (that's us in Britain) needs to do a mental doubletake to understand Murray's identification of writers and farmers as brothers in the primary production trade. Australia has post-modern ruralists – here the few remaining ruralists are by definition traditionalists. The postmodern pastoral, or anti-pastoral, mines rural Australia for its pungency but applies city modes of apprehension. John Kinsella is the best known practitioner but there are others here: Anthony Lawrence, for example.

Generalisations are useful and necessary, but poets are always *sui generis*. A few of the *Landbridge* poets are more likely to find readers beyond Australia than others. Robert Adamson has some fine smoky mediations, especially the night music of 'The Night Heron': "You're just part of the mix, a pain cocktail, dash of white spirit".

Alison Croggon owns a lengthy list of great influences, including Rilke, Bonnefoy and David Jones. Her best poems seem to come from Whitman out of Christopher Smart: "for people go on with the civil business of buying and selling under the hand-written notices" ('The Elwood Organic Fruit and vegetable Shop').

Peter Porter's selection establishes the Australian Porter from the start with 'On Looking into Chapman's Hesiod', which at times you could mistake for Les Murray. Peter Goldsworthy's sequence 'Chemistry' is a series of crisp and witty vignettes: "Beyond this bottleneck / the sum or minus distillate squeezed out / in pure and simple form, the right-hand / side of declaration, arrived at / less by magic than by see-though logic". Gig Ryan mines a seam of tough urban angst: "Loneliness chucks out before me like a rig / its bleak subtext of despair". A fairly safe prediction for the Millennium is that English will be liberated as an international language, and that the often defensive attitude of poets in Britain towards the internationalisation of poetry in English will necessarily fade away.

Landbridge is due to be published in the U.K. by Arc. Through it a wide range of Australian poets will become part of the currency of poetic discourse than ever before.

Landbridge: Contemporary Australian Poetry, edited by John Kinsella, Fremantle Arts Centre Press, $19.95
ISBN 1 86368 269 4; UK edition forthcoming from Arc.

BREAKING DOWN THE BARRIERS

BY JOHN KINSELLA

THE "SPECIAL ISSUE" is an interesting concept. It has a twofold message. First, that it is out of the ordinary, and second, that it is a significant event. The relationship between Britain and Australia is a specific one, though one that has fundamentally changed, and will continue to do so over coming years. As Australia moves towards a republic, and the inevitable displacement of the Queen as its head of state, there is a consciousness both in Britain and in Australia that "difference'" is increasing. But this is an odd way of looking at things, since difference was always there. And the question of a paternal relationship *vis à vis* the colonial and the centre is one that was, at least in theory, ended by Federation, if not before.

Some years ago I co-edited a special double issue of the American journal, *Poetry*. The dynamic was different, as one would expect. The relationship of the US with the English language has similarities to Australia's relationship with English. The question of national language and identity is one that has been worked over time and time again. Australian poetry was presented on that occasion as having certain historical and cultural elements in common with the American, but also as another grouping of poetic voices in an international context. With this issue of *Poetry Review*, these factors are also evident, but the centre-fringe binary is far more obvious and present – it's the uneasy and complex relationship between the "old country" and "new country".

In Australia, the question of cultural sovereignty, of the "vernacular republic", to use Les Murray's expression, of Macquarie English, informs much of the literature of national identity. What increas-ingly makes Australian poetry different from canon-ical British poetry? There are the different building blocks, the different environment and social concerns, and so on, but more than that, the way language itself is changing and consequently alter-ing the way Australians think about themselves with respect to the rest of the world. As with the States, the importance and relevance of non-English language cultures is an evolving focus. The recogni-tion that there are "unofficial" literatures, that Australia's voices are multicultural and not so easily pigeon-holed, is paramount. Of prime importance is the relationship between settler or invader cultures, and indigenous cultures. The framing of these relationships is especially complex given that gradations of rights of presence give rise to other forms of racism and exclusion. For example, the Hansonite voice of anti-Asianism being linked with anti-Aboriginal sentiment. Lyn McCredden's excel-lent piece here explores the growth of an Aboriginal English-language poetry of protest and commu-nity and humour, of relationships to "the land" and white culture specifically.

The question of isolation is being turned on its head in Australian society. Apart from increasingly efficient transport, communications – especially the global village of the internet – we are asking, from what, indeed, is one being isolated? More pollution than we have, ideas that belong to different geogra-phies and histories? There is a growing sense that presence in the now is as relevant and productive as living in a state of mind elsewhere. In recent times I've been developing a theory of "international regionalism" – a global interaction while retaining and protecting regional identity. I think much of the work contained in this issue supports this world view. Australia as national concept is there – even external views of Australia – but it's also there in an international context. This is not a culture looking for security, but one confident to embrace and explore other literatures and cultures without minimising the worth of its own. But it's also increasingly aware of its own failings – of racism, of gender inequality, of the need to stand alone and yet still be an active player in world affairs.

Further, there is the question of the environment. Paradoxically both robust and vulnerable, the Australian environment has been severely affected by European farming practices, logging and mining. Glen Phillips in an article on landscape and contemporary Australian poetry examines some of the ways Australian poets deal with this legacy. There are voices of criticism; there are also voices of celebration. All are part of the picture. And there are the voices of the urban landscape – most of Australia's population is concentrated in its capital cities. Rod Mengham's deft consideration of some aspects of the poetry of John Forbes, Gig Ryan, and John Tranter – poets whose work arises out of the great metropolises of Sydney and Melbourne, as well as an often ironic relationship with the Western tradition – is to be savoured.

In his inimitable ironic style, John Tranter captures much of this Australian take on internationalism in an article on his internet journal *Jacket*. It is evident too in many of the poems. Peter Porter is an interesting focal point, in that he is still seen by some as an Australian poet in cultural exile. But I think his time of "exile" has passed, and he, at least to my generation, is an Australian poet who has made a life abroad. And why not? – he can only enrich the culture he has physically left by feeding it information about the one he has chosen to live in.

It is especially pleasing to see something of a cross-generational representation of Australian poetry in this special issue. There's Frank Kermode's choice of A. D. Hope, one of the few Australian poets of his generation to be known outside Australia. And Judith Rodriguez writing on Hope's near-contemporaries, the brilliant Judith Wright and Gwen Harwood. Plus two fine poems

> This is not a culture looking for security, but one confident to embrace and explore other literatures and cultures without minimising the worth of its own.

from the great senior poet still writing in Australia, Dorothy Hewett. Equally pleasing is the breaking down of barriers. Australian poetry has been fraught with division, especially in the '70s and '80s, but I see that split as gradually passing. The camp of Les Murray and the camp of Tranter-Adamson, or what Murray might once have referred to as the "Balmain poets", are less decided now. People like Peter Minter, Alison Croggon, Coral Hull, Tracy Ryan and Louis Armand belong to no "camp", and have wide-ranging influences and "allegiances". They might read Philip Larkin and Lyn Hejinian on the same evening. French or Korean poetry in translation or the original, linguistically innovative or canonical four-line stanzas: all are in the mix. This issue features two prose poems from Croggon and Hull. Form is active and negotiable right across the board of Australian poetry. I have long seen Les Murray as an innovative user of language. John Tranter himself might be bemused if told he was head of a camp. His efforts through the medium of the internet have done much to break down barriers and divisions. And he's always been a Sydney poet willing to visit Melbourne!

Finally, it is worth noting the increasing availability of Australian poetry in Britain. Apart from editions of Peter Porter, Les Murray, Chris Wallace-Crabbe, Judith Wright, Gwen Harwood, Dorothy Hewett, Dorothy Porter, and myself, there has recently been publication of Robert Gray and John Tranter, with editions due from Bloodaxe of Tracy Ryan, Kevin Hart, and a multiple volume that will include Gig Ryan, John Forbes, and John Scott. Arc also have a healthy Australian list pencilled in for the next few years, as well as the anthology *Landbridge*. But in addition to the publication of Australian poets in Britain, it is my hope that more titles of contemporary British poets will become available in Australia. And of those poets who would not normally find circulation, since they are not published by major companies. The co-publication of J. H. Prynne's *Poems* by Bloodaxe, Fremantle Arts Centre Press, and Folio (Salt), is just one such example. May there be more cultural exchange between the nations, without the prejudices and discomfort of the past. Each has something to offer the other.

The Galah and The Wren

EXTRACTS FROM AN INTERVIEW BETWEEN PETER PORTER
AND JOHN KINSELLA WHICH TOOK PLACE IN MARCH LAST YEAR

JK: We'll just begin with a few general questions. It's your seventieth birthday on February 16th 1999, Peter, you have a collected volume coming out which will collect all your volumes with some new material. Can you chat about that?

PP: Yes – I've done very little suppression, my motto is "Hanged for a sheep, not for a lamb" and I've taken what was in the original first Collected which came out in 1983, so that would be exactly sixteen years ago when the new one comes out. I've more or less reproduced everything that was in the first Collected, in Volume I of the new Collected. Then the second book which will be dated 1984–1999, will consist of all the other books up to *Dragons in their Pleasant Palaces*, plus a new section of completely new poems, called *Both Ends Against the Middle*, about thirty odd poems. Each book will therefore contain something like about 400 pages.

In the second volume I have omitted a few poems from later books which seem to me very questionable, but I have done very little pruning, I've done almost no rewriting, and I haven't even done much slaughtering – in a Herodian manner – of the innocents. So in 1999, practically what could be called my "testimony" will be there in these two volumes of the *Collected Poems*. I might point out for those who already consider me far too productive, to the point of loquacity, that I have at home a collection of unpublished poems about three times as long.

JK: When you say you haven't done any rewriting, and there's a relatively small amount omitted, how do you view someone like Robert Graves who rewrote substantially.

PP: Well, I have a number of views, some of them just amount to laziness or unwillingness, like the dog does not revisit the scene of its vomit or the murderer the scene of his crime, but it's more than that really. I think there's something curiously self-regarding about looking at your work as though it were a canon, a canon already as it were imperishably established, or which you have to make an imperishable establishment of. And it fits in with certain people's personalities, and it fitted in very well with the personality of Graves, but I was looking through my collection of Graves the other day, and I realised that I have lots of different "definitive collections" of Graves. At each particular moment he seems to have regarded that issue as definitive, but they clash, and they are by no means convincing ramifications, they don't help the reader.

There's a lot of great poetry by Graves which he seems to have abandoned, a lot of rather poor poetry which he seems to have esteemed. I think a writer is entitled to do what he likes with his poetry – I mean Auden did some tinkering in a fashion which I don't approve, which I call removing the detonators. Nevertheless, every person is entitled to do exactly what he wants with his own work, but he's not entitled, unless he really is able to do so, to suppress work, or to stop people from looking at other versions which he has propounded and which are available still.

JK: Has there been much editorial intervention, not only in this work, but in your volumes over the years, have you worked with one editor?

PP: No, there has never been any difficulty with my editorial connections whatsoever. My first three books were published by a small publisher in Lowestoft, or the first one was actually Northwood in North London, called Scorpion Press, and they never interfered with my choice for the books; they never even suggested. In fact, in some ways it is good to have some editorial injection. I remember Ian Hamilton telling me once that the trouble with being at Faber is that no-one ever suggested to him that he should leave anything out or put anything in, and he interpreted this that they weren't interested. I have in the past with my publisher's editorial directors had a little toing and froing. I actually welcome that, particularly with my present publisher, Jacqueline Simms, who has been with me – or perhaps I should say, I've been with her – ever since *The Cost of Seriousness*. We do a bit of horse-trading, and I allow her to expel poems which are hopelessly obscure, and she allows me to put poems in which are hopelessly obscure. She tends to want poems which are more readily understood, I tend to want poems which are dark and oracular, but between the two of us, it's like Jack Sprat and his wife.

JK: How important do you see the actual artifact, the book as object? Does that have any relevance to you, or is it purely a thing of expediency?

PP: Yes, it has a lot of relevance to me, and I have a feeling, almost like key centres in music, that my books belong in different keys. There are some C minor, there's some F sharp major, and sometimes there are some bowling along in D major or C major. But the thing I feel about them is that, although you don't know it, if a book belongs to a catchment area, a period of say, three to five years, then your mind was going through as it were a different lot of weather from the weather it was going through in the previous catchment area, in the years before that. So when I've come to put books together, I have an instinct for which order the poems should go in, and I have an instinct too to turn the poems from

a random assembly into something I hope would slightly better distil, slightly better cohere. And the result is, I think, that each book has its own particular air and flavour. For instance if you take my collection called *Possible Worlds*, which is not one of the favourite collections of most readers, it's got a quirky, querulous, almost jokey but at the same time quite disturbed tone to it. Whereas if you take what is actually my own personal favourite book of all my books, the one called *Preaching to the Converted*, which goes all the way back to 1972, that has a tone as close as I get to heavy-weight bafflement and strangely self-inventing forms. That book is as close as I can get to being called a modernist poet, I suppose. It's got a tone which I like, it's got big themes and big structures, and therefore not surprisingly it's not popular with most readers. *Millennial Fables,* which came out quite recently, is clearly a book with too much adipose in it, one feels that there's too much there, and it's the one from which I think have cut the most. In the new, second volume of the Collected, there are only two books from which I've cut very much; the other is *The Chair of Babel*.

JK: Which poems? *Millennial Fables* is one of my favourite books, interestingly enough.

PP: I cut the very long poem called 'Clive and Olive', I cut – what else did I cut? I kept some of the ones which are quite obscure, like for instance I'm quite fond of 'The Worst Inn's Worst Room', which is deeply obscure, and 'The Maria Barbara'. But I cut 'The Tiverton Book of the Dead' which now strikes me as unsuccessful. Oh, and earlier on I think I'd cut 'Millennial Rococo' which now seems to me to be just a bit of a show-off mess. I cut 'Goes Without Saying', or was it 'Intents and Purposes'? I can't remember now. But I kept in a difficult poem like 'Trinacrion Etna's Flames Ascend Not Higher', and I kept in a good deal of the book.

JK: There seems to be a strong link between the way you title poems and the way you title books. Is it always an editorial compromise with the editor, or do you always make the decision?

PP: Yes, it is always an editorial compromise, but I have a great love of titles. The great problem of course is that sometimes one conceives the poem and then writes the poem to fit the title, and the poem is an inadequate base for the the title. For instance in the case of *The Last of England*, of course the title is already thoroughly well established by Ford Maddox Brown in his painting. I liked the title, and I suddenly thought, that would make a good title for a book, especially for an Australian who at that time hadn't ever been back to Australia, from the time he left, at least not from the major time he came over in 1954 – And I thought it would be a useful title for a book which was a kind of discontented summing-up of my first years in England, and I wanted also to say that the idea of England is so much better than the reality of England. I wanted to take a stand against what I think was not so well established then but is thoroughly well established now, which is the substitution for a real sense of a country by a hideous distortion which you can sell to the people called "heritage".

So 'The Last of England' was the perfect title for me, especially as in the picture you see a couple of not particularly admirable chaps shaking their fists in anger at the Old Country, as the emigrant boat pulls away and heads off for New South Wales. But when I came to write the poem, I had no idea what the poem was going to say. As it turned out, the poem turns out rather well; it's got a very obscure first stanza and a much less obscure second stanza. I think that the poem is actually worthwhile as a poem, but it only existed so that I could use the title. And I think that this happens in quite a few cases. The interesting obverse of that, or converse of that, is that what most people think is my best book, *The Cost of Seriousness*, has a title which is not particularly good. In fact, when I told my friend Kit Wright what the book was called he said, "Oh my God, it sounds like the title of some dreadful professorial study of Joseph Conrad".

JK: Can you talk about *Living in a Calm Country*, the title?

PP: Well, that, I made that up, that was just my own invention, I thought it was rather a good because I'd been to see pictures in Tuscany. Once a thing's painted it's calm, and I thought, even if it shows a massacre of the innocents, the blade is still lifted, the blood isn't on the floor. I'd been particularly struck by this ridiculous little saint in San Gimignano who lay down on a plank aged fifteen and never got off it again, the saint of the town. And I thought, one's own body, one hopes, will be as calm as possible, and that's the calm country we actually live in rather than the other country. A title ideally should be slightly piquant, also it should be informative, but above all it should have a suggestion of an atmosphere, a suggestion of a feeling for the book. I find that a lot of people like very very drab titles. Whereas I've always gone in for out-of-the-way-titles – even in my very first book, *Once Bitten, Twice Bitten*. It's got titles like 'Syrup of Figs will Drive Out Fear' and that kind of thing. On the other hand I don't go for – I do sometimes but not very often – the completely jokey titles which that very serious poet Wallace Stevens does. I mean 'The Comedian as Letter C' – well that's not I suppose such an obscure title, but a title like, 'Mountains Covered in Cats'. Stevens' titles are decidedly jokey. The poetry's not, but the titles...

JK: You were speaking about – and titles are part of this – what your readers would find pleasing or not. Do you see yourself as having a particular kind of reader, and do you see your "audience", whatever that may be, having changed over the years or in fact changing? And finally, do you see the Australian reception of your work as being different from the English reading of it, or the British reading?

PP: Well, to try and answer those questions in order: I've never had any real concept of who my readers are. I've always thought that they possibly don't exist. I've always felt gratitude to people who've shown interest and I would even, although it may sound almost unbelievable, extend that gratitude to people disliking the books. At least for having read them. Over the years, of course, you do pick up readers, precious few, but you do pick up readers. And you begin to become someone who a particular kind of reader perhaps goes for, and the problem there is that readers themselves are often influenced by shorthand judgments of the kind of poet you are, which also accumulate over the years. For years and years I've been talked of as a social poet and a satirical poet, and the opposite of a lyrical poet, and the opposite of a pastoral poet. I tend to agree with William Empson that everything is pastoral, but I do feel that my reputation in the world has been misplaced, in a way, largely through fairly glib critical summings-up. I would however modify that by saying that over the years I think I've come around to, or people have come around to, seeing me rather like one of those late Latin poets who was basically a discontented philosopher who has no claim to be a philosopher. So I think that things have in that sense got better – but of course the mode in which all your work is received will depend to large degree upon the most powerful part of it. Since my first wife died and laments for her, which were not as many as people thought, were printed in *The Cost of Seriousness*, and then there has been a return to that, even as recently as *Dragons in their Pleasant Palaces*, which contains a poem called 'Anxiety's Airmiles', which clearly has that pattern in it – I've been seen as concentrating on death and bereavement, and that's done something to remedy the perception of me as a sort of journalistic commentator. But of course, that too is not a characteristic mode necessarily.

I don't know whether the poets you admire are the people whose work you will see in your own poetry. I'm a tremendous admirer of Browning, a great admirer of Auden, a great admirer of Rochester, and who does not admire Shakespeare? I like poems of ingenuity, poems of skill, poems of cleverness, poems which use words in ways other than the Wordsworthian "voice of true feeling". In other words, I like poems to have a kind of plot of their own over and above the kind of worthwhile feelings of the poets.

JK: You're sounding almost L=A=N=G=U=A=G=E poet there!

PP: Well, yes, but I think that the trouble with that is that they have such a narrow vision of what that kind of thing is that they tend on the whole simply not to give enough – the bones are all right, but there's hardly any meat to chew on, and there's hardly any marrow in them either – to use a disgusting carnivorous metaphor.

JK: Well, I'm a vegan. How is your work perceived in the U.S.?

PP: Never in America at all. I've only ever had about two reviews in America which showed the slightest interest in me. Let me state bluntly right from the start, I don't exist in America. Oddly enough, someone who now does support me a little is somebody who also gave me the worst review I ever had, and that's the American poet Carolyn Kizer, who once reviewed me saying that I was the very epitome of everything that was bad about modern British poetry. She didn't know I was Australian of course. But then later on she came round to thinking that I was all right as an Australian...

JK: That's interesting, as a British poet you weren't any good, but as an Australian poet you were?

PP: Well, that appeared to be so, she might deny that, I don't know, but that's how it seemed to me. I don't have the right kind of mind for America at all, I don't know why that is. It doesn't seem to go down in America. What does interest me is the way in which my reception in Australia has changed. And it hasn't changed just because I've been there more frequently and made friends with people, and I'm now seen to have been all along an Australian, and not just a renegade Australian living in England. There has been a more genuine appreciation. And in fact curiously, it is the Australian critics and Australian reviewers who have led the way in seeing my poetry as intellectual and philosophical rather than as social and satirical, as the English have seen it. The English have seen me either as a social-satirical poet who laments elegiacally death and family and that sort of thing, but the Australians see me almost as an ideas poet, and I always have to stress firmly that poets are not philosophers. I detest philosophy. I think philosophy as such is so codified that it is unworthy of the attention of an intelligent person. And that therefore what poets do is think. Thinking and philosophy don't seem to me to be the same thing at all. And I think that Australian critics have on the whole directed the attention in my work to its thinking quotient. I don't mean that my thinking is in any way a purposeful thinking or a systematic thinking, but the fact is that thinking is a passion, and reason, far from being a tool of logic, is another passion. And that therefore to some extent I'm rather grateful for the way at the present moment Australian critics of my work have concentrated on what I think are some of its more interesting aspects, rather more than present-day British critics do.

JK: This sudden rediscovery in the late '80s and '90s of the Porter *oeuvre* has a lot to do with the acceptance that Australian language and literature is part of an international phenomenon, and you're now seen as someone who has helped break down those barriers down for us, so you're actually put in the vanguard.

PP: There's still of course a lot of hostility, not just because I live abroad but also based on the fact that my sensibility is not the commonest form of sensibility amongst Australian writers. I mean, I still get reviews rather like the one Fay Zwicky gave me once years and years ago, where she said, Bring him back to Australia and rinse those cloudy skies out of his eyes and let him live in a bit of Australian sunshine and stop being a miserable, gloomy person. But there are still quite a few people who, to put it at its very best, because I think I respect this, say they just can't see what it's about. I remember reading a poem of George Fraser's, G. S. Fraser, a Scots poet years and years ago, where he talked about going for a job in Glasgow to some vulgar editor of some dreadful newspaper, and he said he could see the editor looking at him and wondering what his sort of person was for. I often feel that in Australia people look at me, they're not hostile, they just think, What is he going on about? The things I write just seem to them to be so remote from what they're interested in that they just shake their heads in bewilderment.

JK: This sort of removal in some ways has proved an advantage. As Australian writers become more conscious of the profound factionalism that has existed in Australian verse, you're actually seen as being outside that factionalism by many. That may not be the case in England, I don't know.

PP: Well, it is and it isn't in England. I started off in England and very few people knew I was Australian. I mean, the clues were in the poems, but they didn't read them very carefully, and so for years and years I was considered completely part of the English poetry scene. As the English have become more and more aware of my Australianism, they've become less and less interested in me, which is the opposite of someone like Les Murray, because Les, and not only him but a lot of Australian poets, can enjoy what I call the exotic attraction. I mean, there's a difference between, you know a galah and a wren. And one bird is more garish than the other, too. So there is that side. But I was never brought in from the beginning as Australian, and the more and more they see me as Australian, the more as more they see me as inferior in Australianness to the Australian poets they've now become aware of.

JK: Once they become aware that this is not what all Australian poetry is about, there will be a reevaluation and valuing of your work in England as well.

PP: Well, fortunately, but there's quite a consider-

able section on my work in Sean O'Brien's *The Deregulated Muse* – a very panoptic view of modern English poetry – and Sean of course completely ignores the Australian side of it, because he only treats me up to about *The Last of England*, and he sees me as an integral figure in this change of emphasis in English poetry which is now his cornerstone. So it would be a whole range of people, like Ian Duhig, Simon Armitage, the new kind of British poetry – of course, it's not the only new British poetry. So there I'm seen as a sort of founding father, and that to some extent goes back, or reinforces the way I was seen when I first started out here. But in between of course – and Sean would be the first to acknowledge this – is the Australian background. It's like show-through or print-through, that the Australianness has come through the later poetry, not in subject-matter necessarily, but that people begin to recognise that my view deviates from that of the standard English. It also deviates from the standard Australian view, but it certainly deviates from the English view. I mean, "Australian" is after all a term which no Australian can bestow on an Australian. The term "Australian" has to be bestowed by someone who is not Australian.

JK: Absolutely, you've hit on the nub of contemporary literary theory, and that is that a destabilizing of a central reading is how we actually develop new language and new poetics.

PP: But I'm really a traditionalist in that sense, and I'm less of a tortured traditionalist than someone like Gig Ryan who's really an avant-gardist but who would like to be a traditionalist. I think I have been held in some suspicion by the more avant-garde. For instance, with the kind of poetry that was being written in Australia, from about 1965 to about 1980, I was certainly *persona non grata* in that period. You wouldn't get many people praising me who were adepts of journals like *The Ear in the Wheatfields* or whatever it was called. You know, Hemensley and all those guys wouldn't think...

JK: You know, this is really interesting, because your biggest supporters during the "years of denial", if you like, by the Australian poetry community re you being an Australian poet, were the so-called "generation of '68", were John Forbes and Gig Ryan and that whole crew. These were the people who always believed in your work, and their common statement was that you were the master craftsman, that you actually knew how to construct a poem, so you were a model, you were a poet's poet during that whole period.

PP: I used to have great arguments with John Forbes about how far technique in poetry was visible. I used to sometimes say to him: John, you can't go all the way with O'Hara, you can't really in the end elevate that concept which the academic critics called *sprezzatura*. You can't take the gentlemanliness which at one time was a gentleman's gentlemanliness and now is insouciance based on a superiority of gesture. I said, that's all very well if people know that your sort of lightness is the lightness of a highly intelligent, well-informed person. But too many readers are only going to see the lightness, and they're not going to see... Too much jokiness, and too much flimsiness, ceases to be stylistic and it just looks like a worn-out old sheet, you can see through it. And I used to rebuke John, I said, "For a man of your fastidiousness and your ability, you don't actually allow the technique to show in the poetry". Now, you could say that was a good thing, you should never have technique showing, but I'm not sure of that. I'm not sure that it is such a good thing. And I think sometimes some of John's more casual pieces are so casual they just look like anything somebody might have scribbled on the back of a menu. Therefore I am a bit inclined, I admit, in a rather heavy lucubratory way to like the wrestling to be visible.

*   *   *   *   *

JK: How do you apply the principles you've developed over the years of writing to the process of anthologizing? How do you apply it to selecting other people's work? How much does a cultural framework, how much does a reading of a culture affect your work? Or how much is it literally applying these rules to each poem in its own right?

PP: I think one kids oneself. I am a far more biased person than I ever want to admit. But I have got one feature which I consider – though other people may not – to be a redeeming feature, and that is, that I rather like the things that are not like me, I rather like other people's flowers, as it were. And I often find myself attracted by things which appeal directly to a sense of pleasure and jump the hurdle of a stylistic sympathy or understanding. I think that's probably what Eliot meant in his slightly over-quoted phrase, "A poem may communicate before it is understood". I would even go further and say that a poem is never fully understood, though it is often fully appreciated. I think that an anthologist of course can never be totally free of bias. What he will do is that he will try to allow the pleasure principle to do his selection for him, rather than any abstract or moral or philosophical or stylistic guideline outside his taste. In other words, curiously enough, an anthology based on one's taste is less exclusive than an anthology based upon any specific set of co-ordinates which are built in to a cultural view.

JK: I'd like to discuss your *Oxford Anthology of Contemporary Australian Poetry*. If you look at Les Murray's anthology, there is quite specifically a politics at work there, he trying to present a certain national "identity" of Australia.

PP: Well, I'd say yes and no to that. I think that's true of his selections from about the First World War onwards. I think his selection of the nineteenth century is brilliant.

JK: I agree.

PP: Because his taste there enables him to escape what is the curse of looking back on emergent literatures or emergent civilizations: the curse of Fustian, the curse of selecting things because they were the best at the time, the curse of selecting things because one wants to honour pioneers. And I think there Les has shown fantastic taste. A good example is that he chooses from Henry Kendall a remarkable poem about that obscure wind-battered island in the southern Indian Ocean called Kerguelen. It's an extraordinary piece of Swinburnian writing. It could almost be a piece of Swinburnian hendecasyllabics. And he spotted it. He's also spotted, not in that anthology but in his religious verse anthology, I think almost the best poem that Kenneth Slessor ever wrote, which is the one about the Reverend Samuel Marsden. It's a superb piece of Calvinist rhetoric. I think Les has got natural good taste, but when he gets closer to the present it tends to get overwhelmed by his polemic and by his special pleading. He's like the Wise Men following a star, except it's taking him into an unwise place.

JK: That's a great line.

PP: I tell you what's wrong with my anthology, it's quite simple: I didn't spend enough time on it, because they didn't offer me enough money, and I didn't have enough facilities. I am not an academic, I have a lot of faults, I come out into a rash if I go into a library, I loathe the gathering –

JK: Before you demean the anthology any more, I should say that I think it's an excellent non-partisan anthology of contemporary Australian poetry.

PP: It would be better if I'd been able to read more books.

JK: That may well be true, but in terms of its aesthetic it doesn't discriminate against types of poetry.

PP: No, it doesn't.

JK: Did it help being both an "insider" and "outsider" in terms of the Australian poetry community? Being physically distant? In some ways it was a disadvantage in terms of not being able to get hold of certain material, but maybe from the point of view of selection?

PP: Well, in retrospect, it might be considered an advantage. At the time it felt like a hideous disadvantage. And it was also done in spurts, that is, from the time it was first commissioned until the last big flurry to get it ready for the press – and I couldn't extend it any longer – sometimes a whole six months would go by without my adding a single person to it. It's swings and roundabouts – I had read a lot of Australian poetry, not as much as some people have, but more probably than some people who teach it in universities. On the other hand, I have to earn my living by paying journalism, and so consequently there are long periods when I simply can't spend time doing the thing.

My attitude towards styles also changes from time to time. I think that by the time I was finishing the anthology, I was a good deal more open-minded than when I began it. I think I began, not as counter-reformation, not with a traditionalist urge, but I think that my view of Australian literature was more traditionalist, until I began to read more widely in it, when I began to appreciate in fact that it was full of rather audacious writers. I would rather use the word audacious than experimental. And I was struck by how original and clever and strange some of the Australian poets were. Therefore I was rather pleased when it got reviewed by Robert Potts in the *TLS* saying that it contained more poems that he liked than any other anthology that he'd read for a ling time. He even said it made him cry.

JK: That was the Dennis Haskell poems, he said it brought tears to his eyes.

PP: In some respects, it opened my eyes, as well as opening the eyes of some readers perhaps, as to how much idiosyncratic good writing was being done in Australia. And I would stress the idiosyncratic. Because Australian writers seem to be needful of jerseys to wear, you know they have to belong to this group or that group, it's only when you get down to it do you realise – and I imagine that someone like Forbes would be the first to agree with this – that they are an idiosyncratic bunch. They don't actually wear those jerseys so comfortably.

JK: And those jerseys don't fit anywhere else in the world.

PP: No.

JK: You've done quite a few anthologies, *New Writing* and others. Did you take that experience into this anthology, or was it entirely separate?

PP: Oh no, they're not entirely separate. Some of the people I admire are great anthologists. The late Geoffrey Grigson is my ideal of a really good anthologist, widely ranging, very bigoted in some respects, but able to overcome his bigotry because of the sheer expanse of his sympathies in intelligence even if not always stylistically. And I think that anthologies of the past are always easier to do. It's notable, for instance that in the Oxford book that Les Murray did, which covers of course the whole of Australia's history from the foundation to the present day, unlike mine which only goes from 1945 to the present day, that Les becomes very uncomfortable the closer he gets to the present day, because he finds it harder to cope with his strong sense of... I mean, for all he's Roman Catholic, he's actually part of Cromwell's New Model Army, and he's always putting on his steel breastplate and going out to fight, not for Cromwell's God but for the Catholic God. And in some ways this makes him extremely unfair to many of his contemporaries.

JK: In your introduction to the Oxford anthology you talk about your reasons for starting at 1945. Do you want to say a bit about that?

PP: Well, prejudice really. Because I thought – I found out in reading that this was wrong – but I thought there had been so much rather bad verse written in the first fifty years of the century, that it was nicer to stick to the present. Where anyway I thought that my ability to judge was rather better. But I also think looking back on it that it wasn't a bad idea, because I do think that the Second World War was – unknown to most Australians today who wouldn't even know when the Second World War was, probably – a great watershed in the country. The First World War was a watershed for the whole of European civilization, by which I mean America and Australia as well. That was the great watershed. But there was a secondary watershed, and the modern world, the world which we now know with its international organisations, multiculturalism, the United Nations, is a direct product of the war with Hitler. That war which brought in also the concept of racial destruction, genocide. And brought with it for Australia a belated sway of nationalism. Australia has always had nationalism. People can point to the turn of the century when *The Bulletin* was maintaining a very nationalist view of Australia. But I don't think that of Australians themselves, and certainly thinking of my family, who possibly didn't like Poms, but who never had any sense that Australia's loyalty belonged anywhere but with the British Empire. And I think in many respects that from 1945 onwards we've entered an Australia which had been prefigured certainly in my early days in the 1930s by the Americanisation of our culture. We'd become completely American in terms of popular culture, though we still remained British in terms of high culture.

JK: Especially in Queensland, where so many American troops had been bivouacked.

PP: That's right, they were there at the time. From 1945 onwards, Australia as it is now seen, both from the good aspect of Australia right through to the Crocodile Dundee aspect of Australia, was born. Other people prefigured it, the Jindyworobaks may have prefigured it, but I think I was right to choose 1945. It did allow me of course also to exclude Slessor, on the grounds that I think that he's far too prominent in Australian literature already. Not that he isn't good, but that he's such a founding father – and this applies even more to Brennan, who I don't think is much good at all. Australians fall back on Slessor both as an example of someone who's good as a modernist and someone you can trust

as a bloke, and I think in many ways that has misled a lot of people.

If we had to have one Australian poet who I think is a real founding father of Australian verse, I would not choose Slessor, I'd choose Francis Webb. It seems to me that Francis Webb had another advantage, he was international and he was nuts. He was mad in the sense of being a tortured human being, not mad in the sense of irrational, but mad in the sense that he embodied in himself what I think is the great strain in Australian life. I don't think I could walk down a Sydney street without hearing someone shouting obscenities at me. Now London is a very mad city. Big cities are mad. But there's a sense in which Australia is an edgy country, a very unsettled country in the mind, not unsettled on the land. And I think that post-1945, we're seeing the emergence, the print of the nation, as it's now at last being printed – in a way that it wasn't in the nineteenth century, that it wasn't in the first half of this century. You might almost say, I think, that Australia begins to be Australia after the Second World War.

JK: Moving on to your most recent book, *Dragons in their Pleasant Palaces*, first of all the title.

PP: I took that from Isaiah, as it says in the book. People don't seem to understand that it means that dragons are eating up the nasty people who live in their pleasant palaces, it doesn't mean that dragons live in pleasant palaces. The "their" refers not to dragons but to us.

JK: The poems in the book follow on from *Millennial Fables*?

PP: Well, largely. There are one or two hangovers, for instance the last poem in the book which a lot of critics have quite liked, the jokey but basically serious poem called 'Death and the Moggy' had in fact been rejected from *Millennial Fables*. I looked at it again and rather liked it, so I put it into this one.

JK: We talked about mortality in your poetry. There's 'The Dance of Death', there's 'Men Die, Women go Mad', so it does have a presence.

PP: But that presence is probably running through my work like Brighton rock, at all points and not just recently.

JK: When it actually came to compiling the book, was this a case where the concept of the book came first and you basically constructed it, or is it one that came later?

PP: Well, for my last three or four books, perhaps

since *The Cost of Seriousness*, I've always been aware that I need a balance between those poems that are centred in Europe, those that are centred in Australia, and then the third category, those that are not centred anywhere except in ideas. 'Men Die, Women Go Mad', for instance, opens with my credo against William Carlos Williams. "No ideas but in things", says William Carlos Williams. And I say, "But things aren't words. And understanding clings to limitation's symbol. The caged bird sings". And so a lot of my poems are based on ideas, because I do believe that an idea has a palpable presence. And I think that Williams is wrong to think that ideas should be replaced by chairs, tables and trees. Or even such other things as there might be.

So the book is really a negotiation – if you look from the way it goes though, it starts off in generalities, with a generalized poem which derives from Kafka – I was reading Kafka's *Aphorisms* at the time that I wrote it – then it goes on to what I'd seen when my cat was being killed by the vet, and also this beautiful marble statue by Stefano Maderno in a church in Rome. It then goes on to Hardy; and I wrote this when I was reviewing that enormously long biography of Hardy by Seymour Smith. Then I was reading Auden's juvenilia. So you can see it starts off in a general tone, then it goes straight on to Australian poems, and two of them are directly written about Canberra, one of them 'Breakfasting with Cockatoos' and the other 'Mobile Pool Cleaner' are both Canberra poems. Then I change again and go back into generalizing. Then we've got a key poem, 'The Western Canoe', which as one reviewer pointed out – it was a very good review by Martin Duwell in *The Australian* – is really a mixture of Harold Bloom's *The Western Canon* and another book – I can't think what it is. The whole idea is a joke, but it ends seriously, in that he manages to quotes in the review quite correctly what the King of Brobdingnag did say to old Gulliver which was, "From your own confession to me, human beings are the most pernicious race of little odious vermin that nature ever suffered to walk upon the surface of the earth".

Then we go on in general, there's a historical poem about the two cultures, which is Dr Leavis's nonsense. And I did actually come across a statue of Fibonacci in the Campo Santo in Pisa. And then I was talking to David Malouf about his trip back to Lebanon, where his ancestors came from, and that more or less gave me 'Dragons in their Pleasant Palaces'. Especially as my daughter at the time was studying in North London University, and I more or less got from her, "Where are the Science Students Gone to media studies?"

JK: Speaking of media studies, one thing that is very noticeable in this book – and it edges towards it in *Millennial Fables*, but it's far more obvious here – are the subversions of popular culture.

PP: Yes, well I'm an elitist in a sense.

JK: But you're playing with it, and very humorously as well, whereas your ironizing in earlier poems tends to twist around more classical...

PP: Yes, perhaps in my old age I'm getting more up to date. 'Fat and Salt' comes from when I was standing in a bar in Durham with a university man, who taught there, and he was an Irishman. And he was eating pork scratchings, and he said to me, "The two most beautiful words in the English language: fat and salt". And then 'Anxiety's Airmiles', I was still thinking of my first wife's death and then 'Miracles' is based upon a trip to south Italy, and then the fact that my wife's younger daughter just had a baby. 'Deaths of Poets' is just a sort of literary fantasy. I love John Ford's work and I didn't like T. S. Eliot's essay about it, so I took that on.

These cultural poems are because I'm fascinated by people who didn't meet up with each other. 'Collateral Damage', there's a full explanation of that in the epigram, that poor old Beethoven was a horrible mess of a man but a great artist. And then there are playful things, like 'The Tenor is too Close', I actually observed this.

JK: This is Porter's notes, this is great.

PP: '...Needlework' is just a joke. I like the fact that what we call the "id", the "ego" and the "super-ego" gives a nasty kind of official tone to it, whereas in German, oddly enough Freud does not use these Latinate words, he calls them *das ich*, *das es* and *das überich*. So he keeps it in the vernacular, which I think makes it rather different, and less fulsome, less forceful. In general, *Dragons in their Pleasant Palaces* is lighter in tone than usual. I feel I am getting more pleasantly irresponsible as I get older.

TWO POEMS BY PETER PORTER
THE REMEDIES

And there beside him in the toils of life
There stood these stalwart helpers, one by one,
Brave Iodine whose tincture on his knees
Brought reddened pain but healed the gravel rash,
hydrogen peroxide, frothy friend,

A further keeper at the toxic gate,
Potassium Permanganate
(Condy's Crystals as personified),
A purple lake, attrition to disease,
Soft Friar's Balsam, smoothest unguent
The semi-sacerdotal remedy.
Internal warriors of many kinds
Were household helpers too – sage Senna, boiled
Or tabletted, cascara, bitter tasting
But good friend to smooth evacuation,
From California a richer syrup
Made of figs, the liver oil of cod,
The same effusion of the Mutton Bird,
The influenza-killers, headache's foes
Given god-like names, Aspro and Bex,
Antiphlogestine poultices, whose hug
Burned pneuma in the tufa of the lungs.

These now were gathered close to wish him well,
His childhood champions who proudly took
Their last farewell of one who'd reached the goal
Of manhood. Household magic, rough and loving,
Now must wave goodbye as on the path

Ahead lay only highly calibrated
Remedies. Though he perhaps might come
Again as prodigal to this same gate
They servant-like bade speed as he set out,
The perfect tint of beauty on his skin,
To meet the blemishes prescribed by time.

MAGICA SYMPATHIA

Lord Herbert of Cherbury
Lounges in a thicket
Like an unplucked strawberry
Isaac Oliver, his pinxit.

Montgomery Parish Church
Keeps all the little Herberts
As terracotta dolls. Which
One is George the Wordsmith?

Magic fills the landscape –
What, here in Wales?
A flowery English handshake
For Llandrindod Wells?

Windfarm propellors' traction
Turns a Lute Book's pages,
Victorian reticulation
Laps Vyrnwy's emerald edges.

Ask the hawks which hover
Over Dinas Vawr's sheep
Who if not Glendower
Talks rivers up from creeks?

Those plush hermetic demons
Who internationalise
Wye and Lugg and Severn
Are worth a latin phrase.

The Past is why the Present
Is packed for the Co-Op –
It is and yet it isn't
That time must have a stop.

O Sympathetic Magic,
Sly fortresses and weirs,
O Forests green and stygic,
The Wit of Passing Stairs!

Lord Herbert gave his castle
Up to Cromwell's men,
He held himself a vassal
Only to song and pen.

High Plains Drifter

GEORGE SZIRTES ON A "LANDMARK IN CONTEMPORARY VERSE"

PETER PORTER

Collected Poems

Oxford Poets
2 vols (404pp and 384pp) £15.00 each

WHO WAS IT who asked: who is Peter Porter? I know who it was who said something about the whirligig of time bringing in its revenges. The answer, in any case, is that Peter Porter is our most energetic, restless, morally driven, and conspicuously intelligent poet. Odd how, stringing these adjectives together – and I have already eliminated a few – feels vaguely Tom Wolfeish. But it is true. It is hard to comprehend Peter Porter in just two or three adjectives. For sheer range alone, we have no one to compare with him. His instantly recognisable work carries elements of Auden, of the discursive Byron, of Browning, of George Herbert, occasionally of Ashbery, perhaps even of Brodsky (whose detached intellectual grandeur Porter distrusts possibly as much as his politics). More importantly, somewhere at the heart of his poems, there is also an exiled Australian carrying the memory of a huge half genteel-half provincial, almost rural country which presents him with a notion of pastoral to be corrected by the works of the Italian masters. It is the friction between these that keeps him moving: Porter as the High Plains Drifter of High Culture. He is in fact a quest poet who is endlessly sceptical of the object of his quest, a lover of high culture who is constantly in a desperate quizzical dialogue with it, someone who distrusts slickness but designates himself at one point as "a philosopher of captions".

The plains over which he drifts are naturally part of Porterland. Porterland contains: most of Italy including painters such as Melozzo da Forli, Piero di Cosimo, Pontormo; all Renaissance cities and their buildings, chiefly churches; architects like Borromini, poets like Leopardi; Italian grand opera, Italian music, Italian landscapes. But Italy does not occupy the entire field. There is Imperial Rome, Republican Athens. There are German operas and lieder, German music generally, particularly Schubert and Bach, German poets and novelists,

French songs, French books, Winckelmann, Berenson... all the apparatus of high culture. It also contains cats, Popes, domestic sorrow, Auden, money, conspiracies, torture chambers, concentration camps, consumer goods, sex, domesticity, agents of political oppression, seediness, dreams of welfare state Britain, corrupt institutions, great tracts of Shakespeare, the Bible and big encyclopaedias, the chatter of history as well as the chatter of the chattering classes.

It does not contain (at least not to any significant extent): football, pop music, erogenous zones, romantic love, Rembrandt's *The Jewish Bride*, anything by Caravaggio, children, theatre, cinema, alcohol, the Princess of Wales, earth, soil, trees and flowers other than in the form of classical bucolics. There are no agricultural implements but neither are there overshot waterwheels. For some these will constitute a lack, for others they constitute merely a broad definition. The feet may tend southwards but the compass is always pointing to the moral north. The governance is liberal, Old Labour rather than New. It will not abide blarney. It will not talk lightly about the People. The People's Porter is a difficult concept to envisage, let alone grasp.

Personally, I didn't meet him until 1972, when I returned to London with a letter of introduction to him. I found him extraordinarily kind, vivacious and sharp, with a far wider range of interests and sympathies than I had imagined. I am *parti-pris*, as they say. But I also want to be sharp and truthful. At that stage he was known primarily as a satirist. The *Penguin Modern Poets 2* volume of 1962 (Amis, Moraes, Porter) contains some of his best known earlier anthology pieces, pieces that define a period even more clearly now than they did at the time: 'Metamorphosis', 'Beast and the Beauty', 'Lament for a Proprietor', 'John Marston Advises Anger', 'Made in Heaven' and 'Annotations of Auschwitz'. These poems can be read against a tapestry of Pop Art properties. Allen Jones meets Ben Jonson. Rauschenberg takes lessons from Pope. Here are Daks suits, Pick of the Pops, the *Daily Express*, Sark and Ibiza, Conde Nast, Heals and Harrods, chickens on electric spits in shop windows. At the same time, in 'Forefather's View of Failure', in 'Phar Lap at the Melbourne Museum' and in 'Ghosts', we feel the harshness and hopes of colonial life: the Scottish textbook, the war memorial, Bradman, Ned Kelly, Parents' Visiting Day, the Canberra Temperance Hotel. Elsewhere again, there is the characteristic sweep through world politics and the demons of history. These elements persist through all his work but do not wholly define it. The engagement with Italian art and German and Italian music begins to emerge in the seventies and remains. There are the tragic, occasional, more formal laments of *The Cost of Seriousness*. There are talking poems and there are highly formal verses. There is the eternal playfulness.

There is, above all, the refusal to believe in his own solutions. A certain public mode of address is learned from Auden, but is transmitted without the Goethean authority. Porter recoils from such things. What he refers to in 'Talking Shop Tanka' as his "Horatian pleasantries" are yearnings undercut and energised by doubt.

All this applies to the 1983 *Collected Poems*. The second volume of his new *Collected* is, at 384pp almost as thick as the first which is, allowing for some rearrangements – the repositioning of the *After Martial* poems, one of his major works – much the same as in 1983. Since then there have been six books, and a seventh, as yet unpublished one, titled *Both Ends against the Middle*, is appended at the end. That amounts to a book almost every two years. How do these books modify or intensify our perception of his work?

To begin with there appears to be no loss of energy, no mere rehashing of old formulas. Writing isn't merely a habit the poet has got used to. The temperament remains, of course. The work is still driven forward by its dissatisfactions with the world, with the moral order, and with its own facility and downright snappiness. There is no return in subsequent volumes to the grave personal elegies of *The Cost of Seriousness*, which struck such a deep chord in so many people. Porter himself harbours a suspicion that, as with Douglas Dunn's *Elegies*, the reader's feelings in such cases are directed more to the predicament than the poems, which, his honesty prompts him to admit, are no less crafted,

> When someone asks what this adds up to, and whether Porter is a great poet, it is the quality of tension that will provide the answer. The tension must serve to hold the whole vast structure up. Never mind one or two bits of stucco, or the odd plaster putto. Let them fall where they will. My guess is, that once the dust settles, the answer will be that he is.

no less consciously manufactured than his poems on other, less immediately personal, subjects. There is a strenuous determination in Porter to keep life and art apart, or, to put it another way, to be honest to the nature of both, so that the one may comment on the other.

At the same time Porter continues to be a philosopher of captions. There are so many lines that have the force of epigram: assertions, declarations, one-liners, apothegms, it sometimes seems that language exists in order to provide ever more of these. The *aperçus* are delivered, half-proverb, half-slogan. Opening the second volume at random, our eyes light on: "Going backwards can be good" ('Jumping to Conclusions'), "God looks like / anyone who ever lived, but more so" ('Pontormo's Sister'), "All the great composers were heresiarchs / of happiness" ('The Grand Old Tunes of Liberalism'). These lines are mostly in the form of condensed prose statement, standing at a slight angle to the rhythms that drive the poem. Back in 1983 I referred to these, as indeed to elements of the whole vision, as humane astringencies and this still seems appropriate.

The late Porter puts great tracts of the encyclopaedic dictionary to work. His diction, if anything, has expanded, as has his reach from the remote philosophical, art-historical through to the dumb idiomatic. His most recent poems, those included under the title of *Both Ends against the Middle* are richer in rhyme and stanza than many in his previous books, which might suggest that they are light or occasional verse. They are, on the contrary, sharp and dark. "My scary drug was Reason" begins one poem, 'Recreational Drugs', and ends:

> My contrary manoeuvres when I blacked
> My nervous system out in reasoned hope
> Were planned to keep the world of sex intact
> With love on hand as recreational dope

That is lightly said. But the matter is serious. Another poem, 'Sailing to Corminbeuf' considers Yeats:

Time deals with Yeats. But what to do with poetry?
You can stomach-pump vanity from poets
but not from poetry. Blake on the fool and his folly
simply isn't true. It's wiser not to write at all.

And never to die. As for wish-fulfilment,
today I prefer to admire businessmen-artists,

Palestrina, Rubens, Wallace Stevens. Alas,
I'm not like them, I see myself sailing

to eternal life, but am afraid to go to sleep,
I might dream of Yeats, Byzantium, and
Corminboeuf,

I might mistake eternity for somewhere
having no gold or poetry or consciousness.

And in 'Basta Sangue':

> Whatever gathers
> Overleaf is murderous: we move

On through the gallery praising Art which keeps
The types of horror constant so that we
May go about our business and forget.

Porter's art will forget neither art nor the horror.
The new *Collected Poems* is a landmark in contemporary verse. We may remember poets by individual poems or by the nature of their vision and the edifice they erect as a consequence. This is a very big edifice. It is maintained by its central tension: horror on the one hand, art on the other. When someone asks, as they will, what this adds up to, and whether Porter is a great poet, it is the quality of tension that will provide the answer. The tension must serve to hold the whole vast structure up. Never mind one or two bits of stucco, or the odd plaster putto. Let them fall where they will. My guess is, that once the dust settles, the answer will be that he is. And, of course, this is the product of thirty years on the OUP poetry list that was recently described by its chief destroyer, Keith Thomas, as an exercise in "talent spotting" and "creative writing".

TWO POEMS BY DOROTHY HEWETT

CONVERTIBLE

I always wanted a sports car
a convertible   saw myself smelling
of sex & leather
like Emma Peel
hair blown close to the skull
passing a blur of signposts
speeding down freeways

but I never made it
Zephyr   Valiant Falcon
kids & junk & luggage
stationwagons designed for the long journey
an old Mercedes its emblem stolen
dumped in the lane
a Galaxy from a funeral parlour
sleek black as death a car
to carry me nowhere

but up ahead
over the next rise maybe
it must be there flying through shadow and glitter
my soft top & when it rolls
it will snap your head clean off.

EXODUS

In such a time as this when multitudes
stream out abandoned bombed from ruined cities
grandmothers hobbling babies bicycles
luggage on carts and backs the crying children
there are no boundaries a private grief
shrinks to a pin prick on this frontier
the ditches filled with blood and suitcases
lovers shot through the heart abandoned toys
dragging a severed limb
a three legged dog limps off across the plain

this unmourned multitude who trudge
across earth's thunderous surface
Belgrade to Kosovo to Baghdad burning.

ROBERT ADAMSON

ON NOT SEEING PAUL CEZANNE

Sydney 1999

I think of the waste, years of not believing
the tongue pretending
in the midst of making words

to speak, to keep walking
down along the bend in the road
and cursing myself for not having spoken

The blank sheets of air
that could have been added to
words smudged out and revised with a colour

stroking instead of butting
coming to the shape by layers, stumbling
out from corners and rubbing out the hard light

The countless fish flapping on boards
have they just disappeared
is there no way

of getting them back into the water
to catch again with this new knowledge
with this awareness of the possibility of watercolour

Outside the window in the black night
mosquitoes gather under the flood-lights on the pontoon
until the empty westerly blows

Everything that matters comes together
slowly, the hard way, with the immense and tiny details,
all the infinite touches, put down onto nothing –

each time we touch
it begins again, love quick brush strokes
building up the undergrowth from the air into what holds us

KATE LILLEY

TOLEDO

Each contestant must furnish a condo.
The reading list includes a choice of swimsuits.
Miss Teen USA wins a dark cherry Lincoln convertible.
Congeniality gets a gun shop and a White Castle franchise.

The reading list includes a choice of swimsuits.
Fern hillbillies seldom get their due.
Congeniality gets a gun shop and a White Castle franchise.
The man with a million friends denied himself.

Fern hillbillies seldom get their due.
I knew you were a decent person straight away.
The man with a million friends denied himself.
In convents you try to learn how things really are.

I knew you were a decent person straight away.
"I hate you", Brenda shrieked, "and so does Pedro".
In convents you try to learn how things really are.
As a last resort the fixed income universe.

"I hate you", Brenda shrieked, "and so does Pedro".
You don't want to drive all night for a piece of chocolate.
As a last resort the fixed income universe.
Under hypnosis blue entered her closet.

You don't want to drive all night for a piece of chocolate.
Each contestant must furnish a condo.
Under hypnosis blue entered her closet.
Miss Teen USA wins a dark cherry Lincoln convertible.

CORAL HULL

BLACK ICE AND FROZEN RAIN

in Canada they call it black ice, it falls as frozen rain and ices over
the roads, the great transnational highway is slippery and hazardous,
black ice is the wet equivalent to Australian bulldust, it conceals, it
flurries, it snows, Canadian writers write about ice and winters, I
catch a cold and stare longingly out of the window, it is a squirrel
with a pine cone in its mouth shooting straight up a pine tree, it lifts
the cone that has fallen from the tree back up into the branches, this
is the squirrel's labour, a pine tree, pencil thin it grows into the sky
as much as it grows into the land, I thought the animals were clichés,
straight from children's story books, but here they are suddenly real,
going about their own northern hemisphere private business, like the
first northern hemisphere sunrise, its frozen rising viewed from the
plane, I knew the sky as foreign, the sea and clouds, I desired its
light quicker than it could be given during late autumn, in Australian
schools we learned more about these North American animals than we did
our own, and somehow when we grew up we knew nothing about either, we
know that bears are frightening and that kangaroos hop, and that now
they are all endangered so we switch off, and everytime a Canadian talks
about wildlife, it sounds like a commentary on one of those
documentaries, and I want to know what the trees are called: fir,
spruce, pine, maple, aspen, evergreens past the snowline, then I'm
pushing my luck with the round river stones, come to rest in my palm
next to a local who says, "it's rock okay? It's a goddam rock!" but what
kind of rock? I want to receive its knowledge, it's a Canadian northern
hemisphere rock to be sure, all the magnetic fields inside the rock are
in reverse in my palm, like the basin water going backwards down the
plugholes and drains, what kind of rock really rests here? where is it
from and what slow habitats did it smooth its sides past? how many
stony creeks, rivers, lakes and settlements? I feel twenty five percent
of the world's fresh water supply in its cold crevices, Canada your
forests are watching me from the bus and are worth watching in return,
hundreds and thousands of Christmas trees, in valleys and wildernesses
of Christmas all year round, this is Christmas country straight from
Australian carols, populated by hibernating bears and the loons have
gone south for the winter, so while I'm here I'll never hear one, and
when I say 'I'm after something' or 'It's on the blink,' they don't know
what I mean, I called a blue jay a cardinal, it may seem close but it
wasn't, and then some shaggy white mountain goats crumbled some big
rocks down onto the road, and there were solid brown elk grazing along
at the sharp base of the mountains, I didn't see them at first, but

sensed something huge and gentle in the undergrowth, her enormous shy
head and fierce brown eye, well back along the distance of the face, as
watchful as ever, velvet ears twitching like radar's, this is the face
the hunter looks into before he is sprayed with blood, the hunters
create pulp from the character of the elk, here where the air is thick
with snow, altitude 5000-ft above sea level, it's giddy short of breath
thin aired country, its light green skies are watery and barely warm,
there are the long dry stretches that make me homesick, but this is an
icy desert, the mountains are something we must always look up to, they
are towering down from every direction, their changeable weather is just
behind them, solid rock yet cyclonic inside, they have a presence on a
full moon or just before snow, but I don't know what they are trying to
say, how is the snow in Australia different? well, we have grey
kangaroos hop through it and snow gums and hooked beaked parrots, I
guess the snow in Australia smells like eucalypt, a gum tree, have you
smelt eucalyptus oil? Australia smells like that

KATHERINE GALLAGHER
JET LAG

I didn't go round the world. It went around me
crossing time zones in my sealed-off balloon,

following inflight-arrows across Europe, Asia,
Australia. Don't ask what day it is –

my body clock ticks in those concertinaed
intervals between borders and continents,

oceans urging them forward.
I can't find sleep. Instead I have birds

crisscrossing the lanes of my head.
They saw my airship slip by and me peering

through a window, setting my watch
by the stars. I'll catch up with this shaky life

yet, wrap it around me like a quick nap.
Leonardo put such problems on hold

with his *ornithopter*, needing wings
to bird-flap, before it could move.

No wonder it took centuries
to get off the ground.

Now, just sleep on the possibilities.
I'm still thirty thousand feet up,

nudging clouds like a sunset. The day's
slipping through my fingers.

TRACY RYAN
TWO VIEWS

IN BEADS
The rings of age that will never reach her
settle already around
her neck. Iconic begets *beautiful*
more sixties than herself. His choice. Beads
strung out & hanging as the hours
she made them in, yoke, circle
draping the breast at first unnoticed. Regally
swaddled, a marble baby. Stare me down.
Overpower the gaze in.
Ring, bauble, sequin, nipple,
single eye.

IN BEADS ONLY
Always one step further than asked for
& yet she kept them. Fronted
like a brace of medals. He protested:
a visible line from the just-shed
clothing. Hands fan without discretion
what's hers alone to keep or
give away. Forget the costume.
Bead and flesh are fused,
breast identified: there is no Janis
but this.

S. K. KELEN
EXTREME ORIENT

A barge adrift the Perfumed River –
reclining beneath a parasol
is the courtesan Tigress waving her fan
– barge floats past village and pagoda,
houses and huts midst bodhi tree
coconut palm, flame flowers
bamboo forest, and flat green
leaves float in the green river
tangle roots and mangrove.
In the morning she bathed in the river.
Her black lacquer fan:
a butterfly's deep-blue wings
unfold a painting of a courtesan
poised beneath her parasol
keeping the rain off
a barge adrift the Perfumed River.
The woman on the painting on the fan
fanning herself reposing on her divan
rocked by the river's rice green water,
The farmers move water in the fields,
harvest love songs
to give the famous courtesan
who sees them with affection –
now she has her letters to attend,
the afternoon for reading and to practise English.
The rice rivers rock gently her divan.
Below deck is red silk and velvet bed,
a glass case shelving bottles of shampoo
from every country, freshly folded towels –
calendars signed by football stars
grace the chamber's walls
and glowing with river's love
her very odalisqueness –
she can sing the radio love tune
like a goddess, as strong as any warrior
lay serenely the river's quiet, raindrop plash
the same scence painted on her black lacquer fan
as the fan she is painted on –
a courtesan beneath parasol reclining on a barge
rocked by the gentle river.

She sees pirates from the ocean
come up the river in the eyes of business men –
they sing from the banks of the Perfumed River
she is the one the tigers regard and carp swim after,
her fan unfolds a silvery painting
of a lady with a fan who from her barge
watches farmers work the land.
It is hot and they toil
all morning – buffalo with moon
horns take a bath in mud – she
watches them from her divan –
the farmers and the buffalo –
she lets fall her fan
and painted on it is the picture,
a woman holding a fan
seated pleasingly on a barge
the rain getting harder on her parasol
and the river starting to flow
attending her letters, she will read in the afternoon
and watch on the land the eternity farmers dream –
her fan like a butterfly spreads its wings
to reveal a courtesan who lets fall her fan –
it keeps going, fan after fan a deep-blue butterfly
unfolding the painted scene – on the river a barge
where, shaded by a parasol is the lady
watching the same lovelorn men
harvest rice songs, the fan opens another
and another – fans within fans until the fan
where, in the picture above the courtesan
and the painted scenery
right up in the sky, an old spirit man
rides the clouds in a bathtub,
and plays a harp sparking thunderbolts
 – a mischievous being powerful in the hands
of a courtesan – twangs the lightning
as he steps cloud to cloud
painted on the next fan up,
all the way up, up through black lacqered fans
one after another opening,
fans growing as they approach the world
of the lady on her barge on the gently rocked divan.
When he meets her the sky blacks out

he is a cruel storm. Pray Mercy
bless us with goddess tears on the Perfumed
River – hold back your blessèd typhoon.
The courtesan snaps shut her fan,
swarms of deep-blue butteflies and black moths
are drawn to her light
the river waves rock gently her divan.
A barge adrift the Perfumed River –
reclining beneath a parasol
is the courtesan Tigress and her fan
 – barge floats by village and pagoda,
houses and huts saluted by bodhi tree
coconut palm, flame flowers
bamboo forest, and flat green
leaves float in the green river
tangle roots and mangrove.
In the morning she bathed in the river.

PETER MINTER
LIZARD ARABESQUE

At the end of
the yearning stone,
enflamed

by the prodigy of hell,
your skin is
another day of words

warming, clear
and deep as you wake me.
Look, you will say

at this stone!
Presence renews itself!
turns out

the limit of air
in the body,
paraphrased by shadow.

I repeat everything,
over the fence, over the river,
the tail lost *is a sign of beauty.*

Waiting, the lizard
is still, a small pulse
in the neck

audible here
expands and contracts
to surrender myself again to the earth.

PETER GOLDSWORTHY
BED

With age you learn to love it
for itself and not the company
it keeps. The hint of coffin
in the clean cool sheets becomes
a plus, the tugging up of quilt
is suddenly a joky nailing down
of lid. Even when the eyes slide
shut, this too, becomes a wish:
the little daily death of sleep
beaming us forward in time,
if not, this time, that far.

JAN OWEN
THE KASHAN

You're at the keyhole to paradise
rapt, reluctant, and it's staring back:
breathe in its gaze like scent,
a track down violet and indigo's
twelve by eight blueprint for bliss.
Dexter and sinister conjoined
lull you into the maze.
The design becomes you,
wear it like desire
whose doubling back and forth
is perfume, deja-vu.
These are the gardens of the infinite
where chaos and harmony ravel their sum
till Mandelbrot's sped buds bloom,
fragrant as almond bread from Samarkand.
So what's the recursion for sky spilt
over sand and what transforms
each glint to hologram?
Why do I think of chain-mail rusty with blood,
wool wrung from Tyrian purple in a pail,
two eagles against the sun?
Imagination builds on shifting ground,
pilfering stuff from the past
which steals it back.
Is self or art the parasite?
The commerce between's like
the shimmering sex of light
or how we pulse from particle to wave
short-changing be with have,
ghostly offspring of chance
and a small star patch.
Yet there's this rug's blue map for the trip
and the way we keep packing
love and sadness and shame
so hopefully into the family's one suitcase,
this quantum of time.

THE SONNET HISTORY

JOHN WHITWORTH
BUNYAH WIZARD

"Gummy!" said Beetle. "What a sentence!"

From Mungaroona to Wooloomooloo
To Dubbo, Buggaribbee and Geelong,
Bounding from billabong to billabong,
Aboard his lofty, lolly kangaroo,
One swaggering swagman scourge of the obscure,
Bald as a bandicoot, redneck as the rose
Of poetry – and, starve the bleeding crows,
That stuff's as rare as rocking horse manure –
One of the boys who stole the funeral,
The funeral of poetry, that is,
Big Les in shorts, as does the biz from Oz,
Where you can make a life of hanging loose,
Where mountains answer to the name of Bruce,

The only outback's Emperor of sprawl.

Too Much in Life

SEAN O'BRIEN ON LES MURRAY'S "LIBERTARIAN HYBRID"

LES MURRAY

Fredy Neptune

Carcanet, £18.95
ISBN 1 85754 337 8

"A VERSE NOVEL": now there's a phrase to make the heart sink. It evokes a work with the virtues of neither of its components; for the author, the triumph of stamina over wisdom; for the reader, of duty over desire. Les Murray has already undertaken one such project, *The Boys who Stole the Funeral*, which was strange and interesting but afflicted by Murray's political bugaboos. That was a haiku, though, compared with *Fredy Neptune*, which is not simply a long narrative but an epic. It is also far superior to the earlier work.

Fred Boetticher/Boetcher/ Boytcher/Butcher/ Buttikher/Beeching/Beitcher/ Beotischer (there's also a character called Golightly, as well as a psychopath called Sweeney) is a German-Australian merchant seaman. In the early stages of the First World War, by one of the accidents that propel him through history, he ends up on a German warship. In the Turkish port of Trabzon (more famous as Trebizond) he witnesses an atrocity – the burning alive of a group of Armenian women by a mob. It seems at first that through a combination of shock and helplessness Fred has contracted leprosy, but his condition turns out to be the more mysterious loss of all physical sensation. His illness leads him to the "yellow indoor cemetery" of a leprosarium in Germany, before he escapes. It is part of his peculiar gift to ricochet between and around the century's major events, so that, for example, when his American-bound ship is in the Channel, the cook, watching a ferry full of soldiers making for France, speaking from experience, remarks: "*They going / to camp in the rain in big sewers dug through men*". The image of the trench full of the dead is to recur, first in post-revolutionary Russia, then in the Nazi period.

Murray convincingly weds Fredy's omnivorous observations of the world to a perpetual crisis made partly of illness and partly from his aching separation from home and family. As he moves closer to his heart's desire, the world carries it out of sight again. He is always in the right place for history and the wrong one for himself – with the wrong papers, the wrong name, on the wrong side of several oceans, torpedoed by a U-boat, working a circus strong-man or a crewman on a Zeppelin, derided, menaced, a criminal, an innocent, pursued by the authorities, the hoods, the Japanese, cast out by the ambiguous gift that lets him lift cars single-handed and sit down in mid-air. Dubiously enlisted in the Australian army, Fred returns to the Mediterranean in time to meet T. E. Lawrence, who is displeased by the presence of someone as singular as himself. Then it's off again, through the Depression, the rise of Nazism and the Second World War, with intervals of Home Leave with wife and family before being swept up in the next baffling voyage. The implausibilities of Murray's headlong tale are less important than the ferocious energy of the telling and the capacity not simply to register but to relish the particular even as it hurries out of sight. Murray's basic power has always been descriptive. It's as if his imagination had spent its spare time reading a vast universal catalogue of *things*, enabling him to deal matter-of-factly with the unusual and equally, to make the workaday (and the working life) important and involving. There is the outrageous deadpan comparison: "the ship rode the Bosphorus like an iron on shined blue cloth". More elaborately, there is the passage of rapid-fire description of work which concedes nothing to the reader's ignorance – indeed speaks as if to fellow scuffler, with monosyllabic phleghminess:

> I...walked past a steaming black-rafter palace
> called Birdsville Mill, with the blades slinging big
> > logs flat-sided
>
> under rollicking drive-belts. There were ribby hulls
> > chocked up on ways
> all along the foreshore, and fellows adzing tea-wood
> > knees.
> I met the boss and got on
> and was sent to learn the river and the work,
> wrestling, or coaxing, a fifty-foot sternwheel drogher
> under tons of logs along channels never deeper
> Than two fathom, out of bays and crevices,

and swimming ashore with a line when the crabbing
bitch
went aground again, and killing snakes in her
firewood.

The same brisk notation is also used to substantiate more inward and less immediately promising material:

One time [my body] dreamed my body was made of
fire,
not hurting me, but no flesh human could come
near.
It was tough flowing orange, glaring hard gold
out through its buttonholes and gaps; the clothes
weren't affected.

There are probably hundreds of passages worth quoting from *Fredy Neptune*, but none of them reads as a set-piece. The book is unusually short of transitional passages, those flat meantimes while the imagination resupplies itself. In a sense the book is all transition, driven by the desire to arrive, to be cured, to be anchored. It is amazingly ambitious and extremely modest – an epic which is at times an x-rated cartoon, whose hero is an ordinary person on whom history dumps its entire supply of anvils. The other travellers it recalls – Ulysses, Ishmael, Gulliver – are part of its equipment, not cultural selling-points.

Yet at the same time as the book is so powerful and absorbing, it does beg a couple of questions. *Fredy Neptune* is set out in eight-line stanzas with occasional opportune rhymes. Les Murray has suggested that poetic form constitutes a contract between writer and reader, an agreement to meet certain expectations of shape and recurrence. The contract seems a fairly relaxed one in this instance. Though you could count stresses, the rules would fairly elastic, while the stanza itself seems to provide no grammatical barrier or other significant transition, amounting to a pause for the eye rather than the ear. There are obvious analogies between Murray's method and the cinema – speed, copiousness, a certain kind of realism, at times an indiscriminate intensity. The motor is not so much rhythmic as grammatical: necessarily the poem comes back to the first person, and to summings-up before setting off yet again. Perhaps all this is what he means by a verse novel – a libertarian hybrid. It pumps like an artery, with a readability which might enthrall those who never go near poetry.

There's nothing libertarian, though, about the sense of the world which underlies the poem, which is black and crimson pre-modern Catholic, and in which suffering can seem a little too close to aesthetics (though there is little direct reference to religion). Fredy is in effect cursed, on grounds for which "slender" is too assertive a description: the world is a place of suffering. He gets an Old Testament good hiding and cannot feel a thing (though he *knows* a good deal). In due season he is returned to himself, ending with the wry reflection "but there's too much in life. You can't describe it". The tale is much more interesting than the symbolism, spreading itself in a hundred directions, finding its only unity in its sustained energy – which makes the theology it may have been intended to serve seem superfluous to the life of things in themselves.

LES MURRAY
THE HOLY SHOW

I was a toddler, wet-combed
with my pants buttoned to my shirt
and there were pink and green lights, pretty
in the day, a Christmas-tree party
up the back of the village store.

I ran towards it, but big sad people
stepped out. They said over me *It's just, like,*
for local kiddies and *but let him join in;*
the kiddies looked frightened
and my parents, caught off guard

one beat behind me, grabbed me up
in the great shame of our poverty
that they talked about to upset themselves.
they were blushing and smiling, cursing me
in low voices *Little bugger bad boy!*

for thinking happy Christmas undivided,
whereas it's all owned, to buy in parcels
and have at home; for still not knowing
you don't make a holy show of your family;
outside it, there's only parry and front.

once away they angrily softened to
me squalling, because I was their kiddie
and had been right about the holy show
that models how the world should be
and could be, shared glittering in near focus

right out to the Sex frontier.

No More Boomerang

LYN McCREDDEN ON ABORIGINAL POETRY

THE INTRODUCTION BY Kevin Gilbert to his influential Aboriginal poetry anthology *Inside Black Australia* (1988) can be read as vulnerable and anxious about the relationship of aesthetics and politics:

> Rarely has Aboriginal poetry much to do with aesthetics or pleasure or the pastoral views... there is another reality, a reality that could find parallels in the experience of the indigenous peoples of South Africa or Bolivia, or of oppressed populations within the national boundaries of one culture, the Jews in Nazi Germany or the Palestinians in Israel... Many critics of Aboriginal poetry, whether using polite language or digital graffiti, express some difficulty in finding comparisons and parallels. Their solemn enunciation on the aesthetics, the imagery, rhyming and metric patterns, metaphors, lucidity, fluidity, lingoism, jingoism, polemicism, chantism, phenomenalism of the Aboriginal voice, is an assurance to us that the debate will long continue. Of course, there will be many who, not wanting to reveal any overt or covert racism, paternalism, condescension, misconception, self-deception or otherwise to the value of the contribution, will dart like a prawn in a barramundi pond to the safety of antecedents . . . to make comparisons with the indigenous tree and twist it to the semblance of the "tree back home".

Anxious it might be, but it is also apt and humorous criticism, alive to many competing voices. It manages to sum up a current white liberal paranoia about the appropriate discourses in which to venture upon discussion of Aboriginal literature. Further, it pokes sharply at the academic publishing game, with its formalist and politically-correct obsessions. But Gilbert points to another reality, or exigency, that of the interdependence of white critics and publishers, and contemporary Aboriginal writers, and of the potential, along with trivialising or worse consequences, for helpful dialogue: the "assurance that the debate will long continue". He puts it up to white critics – those darting prawns in the barramundi pond – in a way which acknowledges this interdependence while maintaining his own place in the debate. Two moves for white critics are simultaneously delineated and satirised:

formalist discussion running amok, and liberal breast-beating which desires to praise, but has only its own terms with which to laud the Aboriginal texts. But Gilbert is far from closed to dialogue, and his editorship for Penguin of *Inside Black Australia*, for a wide Australian and international audience, is proof of this. Yet it needs to be remembered that for some it is arguable whether such a transcription of mainly oral art into a Penguin volume in English can be anything but a betrayal, both for black poets and white audiences.

But another voice whispers from beyond Gilbert's sharp satire, that of the skilled white poet and critic, unruffled by theoretical debates about what constitutes "literariness", or perhaps too secure in his own opinion of what does constitute "the aesthetic". Writing about Gilbert's anthology, critic Mark O'Connor is straightforwardly "understanding" about some of the failures of the anthology:

> Gilbert's notes reveal that many of his poets have had only an interrupted secondary education. When they fail as poets, their faults are not related to Aboriginal culture, but are precisely the ones found in under-educated white poets: outdated poetic licences and archaic phrases of the "warriors of yore" variety, thumping rhymes and rhythms, McGonagall-style fluctuations of tone, and above all the reliance of abstract declamatory statements. Good poetry tries to convey even its more abstract ideas through concrete images – something the great Aboriginal song-cycles illustrate perfectly.

For O'Connor, politics must submit at all times to the schooling of aesthetics: ". . . the answer to resistance is not to 'turn up the volume'; in poetry a platitude remains a platitude, even though there may be red-necks or self-servers who vehemently deny it". Such white, middle-class, schooled assurance of poetic standards does not dream of different audiences possible for different poetries, even within the one reader. Nor does it ask questions about the universalism of its definitions of "the poetic", including its insistence on good form. All those unschooled Aboriginal poets out there should take note. Either get more schooling, or ask yourself whether you are a "natural poet" like one in the anthology who is praised. The critic here is, after all, interested in "Aboriginal Literature". Here is a hierarchy of values in which politics must be served by (defined by? reliant upon?) aesthetics. No notion of white aesthetics as an active impediment for a range of writers and readers, black and white. No notion of those elements of "good writing" which the critic prescribes – concrete images rather than abstraction, avoidance of platitudes, subtle rhymes and rhythms, "their own poetic voice and range" – being possible stumbling blocks for a range of poets and readers or audiences at this particular time in Australian culture. It is a universalist, dehistoricizing white aesthetics which is being lauded, and one which seems to have little room for notions of "writing" or "textuality" unleashed for a range of audiences, purposes and effects. The critic is aware of this question of audiences, however:

> White readers may sympathise, but they will lack the Kooris' aching need for personal and racial (or national?) identity. They are more likely to ask 'How good are these Aboriginal poets?' 'Can they write about other things beside being Aboriginal?'
>
> (O'Connor)

While the position of this critic may be seductive for some, with its formalist aesthetics and firm idea of "good writing", a position in which most white critics are trained and entangled, the need to break down the monoliths of "white reader" and "aching Koori" must be addressed. The image of the discerning white reader, settling back for a dose of "good" poetry, devoid of the myriad of political questions resonating in and behind every word read, is surely ludicrous. How far can or should readers go, in their separating of aesthetics and politics? O'Connor's arguments, while espousing a humanistic concern with injustice, and the need for resistance, are uncomfortable with anything but aestheticized readings.

However, Gilbert and O'Connor, operating

For O'Connor, politics must submit at all times to the schooling of aesthetics: ". . . the answer to resistance is not to 'turn up the volume'; in poetry a platitude remains a platitude, even though there may be rednecks or self-servers who vehemently deny it". Such white, middle-class, schooled assurance of poetic standards does not dream of different audiences possible for different poetries, even within the one reader.

with distinct though connected models of human subjectivity and aesthetics, are also, interestingly, bound together discursively. Just as the questions raised by Aboriginal aesthetics do not have a single, static answer, but are historical and reader/audience-oriented, the question of subjectivity in their texts also needs to be examined. While O'Connor calls for "freer" Aboriginal poets, individualists who seem somehow to float just above or beyond historical, racial and political constructions, able "to develop their own poetic voice and range", Gilbert sees "Aboriginal poets... identified with the freedom poets of the lately decolonised countries and as a new perception of life around us, a new relation with the sanctity, the spiritual entity and living Presence within the earth and all life forms throughout the universe". Oodgeroo Noonuccal, a pivotal figure in Australian literary and political culture, was formerly known as Kath Walker. In the Bicentennial year she changed her name to Oodgeroo of the Noonuccal tribe, her people centered on North Stradbroke Island (Minjerriba), off the southern coast of Queensland. Oodgeroo published four books of poetry, *We are Going* (1964), *The Dawn Is at Hand* (1966), *My People* (1970) and *Kath Walker in China* (1988), as well as many stories of the Dreamtime, stories and picture books for children, political and historical essays and speeches. Her poetry was often described in the 1960s and 70s as merely "didactic and propagandistic", but Oodgeroo was capable of short-circuiting such criticism: "I agreed with them because it was propaganda. I deliberately did it" (Noonuccal, *Recording the Cries*, 19, cited in Brewster, 96). But consistently, Oodgeroo found ways of refusing the dichotomies imposed upon her work by white aestheticians: aesthetic/political, crafted/naïve, individual artist/spokesperson. For example, she spoke often about "poetic voice" in communal terms. In a 1977 interview she said:

> I'm putting their voices on paper, writing their things. I listen to the Aboriginal people, to their cry

for help – it was more or less a cry for help in that book *We are Going*. I didn't consider it my book, it was the people.

In her poetry, Oodgeroo uses a range of rhetorical and ideological weaponry as she constructs and inhabits what she has called a third cultural reality, seeking the ear of her people and the ear of the coloniser: dialogue, irony, sarcasm, lament, diatribe, protest and rallying cry are all employed. She takes up no one, monolithic position, but attempts to represent the real voices – the lived expressions – of her people. Sometimes this leads to a poetry of seeming defeat and racial disappearance, in such laments as 'We are Going' or 'No More Boomerang':

No more boomerang
No more spear;
Now all civilized –
Color bar and beer.

No more corroboree,
Gay dance and din.
Now we got movies,
And pay to go in.

No more sharing
What the hunter brings.
Now we work for money,
Then pay it back for things.

Now we track bosses
To catch a few bob,
Now we go walkabout
On bus to the job.

(My People)

In these first four stanzas of 'No More Boomerang', first published in 1964, a number of Oodgeroo's characteristic strategies, both rhetorical and ideological, are evident. The short, blunt lines pick up the intonations of Aboriginal speech, a direct, no-nonsense series of statements, and a grim humor mixed with the lament. The Aboriginal here is the victim of colonialism, in its modern, capitalist form, but the victor too is seen as a victim, inscribed by a system which is threatening both black and white. Under this regime, work is alienating and unrewarding. The inheritance of this system is competitiveness and prejudice, lack of sharing and community, shame, mortgages, long hours of work,

all mod-cons which aren't necessarily better, high art elitism, television with ads and the atom bomb:

Lay down the woomera,
Lay down the waddy.
Now we got atom-bomb,
End everybody.

The quirky mixture of down-to-earth, anarchic humor, together with a plea for mercy from, and a criticism of, white society, is haunting. The victim is not simply self-pitying, but abrasive, cynical, and dismissive about what has been gained under civilized colonial rule. What disturbs here are the restless, mixed tones of what is both lament and protest, coming out of the mouth of a victim who won't quite lie down, and who won't settle for the dichotomy them and us, colonizer and colonized. Civilization is attacked as a system – white, capitalist and consumerist – which swallows up all its adherents.

Jack Davis, a Western Australian Nyoongar, is from Oodgeroo's generation and is an esteemed poet, playwright and autobiographer. His poetry collections include *The First-Born and Other Poems* (1970), *Jagardoo: Poems from Aboriginal Australia* (1978), *John Pat and Other Poems* (1988) and *Black Life: Poems* (1992). Davis' poems have maintained both lyrical and political directness. He's sometimes described as Blakean in his simple and highly fraught lyrics. 'Exhibition', from Jagardoo gives a feel for the complex role thrust upon Aboriginal artists in Australia:

They stood admiring Aboriginal art.
Hipshot*, I stood with them
Playing my part.
They murmured, What colour, what line!
I thought, A green sky –
That suits them fine!
It's their eye.
Whose ego was impressed –
Theirs or mine?
I felt suddenly depressed,
But hid my gloom,
Starched shirtfront, overdressed,
Lonely in the room.
(*Hipshot – standing with the weight on one leg.)

There's a wry refusal to "play Aboriginal" here, even as the social self is depicted being pressed into the shapes of postcolonial Australian native artist. This same movement between ironic and lyrical, poignant voices is characteristic of Davis. As Kevin Gilbert put it more forcefully, in discussing First Born: "Jack firmly established himself as an Aboriginal poet shouting, sobbing, demanding that his song, the Aboriginal song against injustice, be heard". In 'Aboriginal Australia: to the others', David does shout against "the brutish years" through which Aboriginal Australians suffered,

> ...Flung into a common grave
> You propped me up with Christ, red tape,
> Tobacco, grog and fears,
> Then disease and lordly rape
> Through the brutish years.
> Now you primly say you're justified,
> And sing of a nation's glory,
> But I think of a people crucified –
> The real Australian story.

Like Oodgeroo, Davis takes on a communal, even prophetic voice which claims the right to speak across the nation, from Western Australia where he lives, about "a people" uniformly brutalised. Amongst the next generations of Aboriginal poets, from those in their fifties and sixties, such as Western Australian Mudrooroo, Queenslanders Roberta Sykes, and Archie Weller, to young and little published Melbourne poets such as kooris Lisa Bellear and Tony Birch, a common thread of solidarity with other Aboriginal peoples is evident, though the ways in which they respond to what some would call the genocide and systematic subjugation of Aboriginal people, differs politically and aesthetically.

One contribution made by Roberta Sykes, a Queenland Murri educated at Harvard, was to open up the debates about being a black woman in Australia. In the anthologised poem 'Black woman', from the 1979 collection *Love Poems and other Revolutionary Actions* she writes:

> Black Woman
> the tears you cry – you are told –
> should be tears of joy
> black women are on the way "up"
> you now must ponder
> who will babysit the kids
> while you make your (un-paid) t.v. appearance
> you must try not to let your bitterness
> be construed as "black racism"
> as you recall the abuses

> heaped upon you all your life
> and you view your "liberation"
> with a scepticism born of poverty,
> corrugated-iron shacks, no water,
> four children from six live births
> and the accumulated pain of two centuries

> black woman black woman black woman black
> woman black.

Again, the strongly communal sense of what it means to be Aboriginal is evident in Sykes work, as in Oodgeroo and Davis, but as well as this, a "revolutionary", 1970s, and possibly American black consciousness can be heard informing the poetry. The pulsing insistence of her free verse is laced with a bitterness found in the presentation of fact after fact: poverty, corrugated iron shacks, no water, infant mortality and hard child-birth. Issues of gender and race are strongly entwined in Sykes' work, and particularly so in her recent, prize-winning autobiographical works.

In the more recent work of younger generation poets, a complex mapping of imperialism, capitalism, gender and class becomes the focus, sometimes moderating the earlier givens of community and unity. In the edgy, not always successful poetry of Mudrooroo, who is better known as a novelist, a postmodern splintering of identity is partly celebrated, partly understood as a wound of racism:

> Lost in the lucky country
> ...I find my clean jeans at the Salvos,
> They throw in a shirt or two,
> And my socks don't stink,
> And my boots have soles,
> To move me from this place to the next,
> With an accent gone awry,
> So that I talk like some kind of wog,
> Once someone even called me "Yank"!
> And I told him quick-smart –
> We own the country now
> So don't get uppity,
> Or we'll bring you to your knees
> And make you all Abos in a new state called free.
> ('Lost in the Lucky Country', from *The Garden of Gethsemane: Poems for the Lost Decade*, 1991.)

The uneasy mix of pride, self-pity and braggadocio, characteristic of Mudrooroo's poetry, makes his verse hard and sometimes exhilarating to read. It startles with its rapid shifts of mood and subjectivity, even as it often sags into cliché or worn language. This rawness and refusal to finesse either the form or the textual state of mind is also found in the work of young poet Lisa Bellear, though there is a more successfully self-conscious level of poetic crafting going on than is often found in Mudrooroo's verse. In 'Souled Out', Bellear writes:

Only $200 – Ladies/
Gents and you could
Become an Aborigine
For two whole days!
Hey lady, what's sar matter
Haven't you seen
One before?
Come and experience
The lifestyles and
Mystical spirituality
That is quintessential
To the life and existence
Of a Traditional Aborigine
We'll also have a real
Properly initiated Elder
Who will empower you
With Dreamtime secrets
From an ancient culture
And for an extra fifty bucks
We'll throw in some
Real live witchetty grubs
And eat them, just like
The Natives did all those
Dreamtimes ago.

(Dreaming in Urban Areas)

There's a feisty, individualistic sense of personal and racial fight in Bellear's poetry, and a sarcastic humour which is just as often self-directed as it is aimed at the "gubba middle-class" and other voyeurs – well-intentioned or not – who seek to define the koori woman speaker's subjectivity and to grasp a bit of Traditional Aboriginal culture. Here and elsewhere Bellear uses slang, sarcasm, humour, name-calling and nostalgia, in a heady, fast moving and highly vocalised performance. Her poetry readings bring out these elements – she speaks to and at the audience, preaches at them, cracks jokes, reads poems, all in a rapid-fire performance which can shock the first-timer.

While Bellear's racial and family background is most recently urban – hence the title of her one collection – the poetry of Lionel Fogarty, a Queenland Murri from the notorious "troublemakers" settlement of Cherbourg, seeks to maintain links with tribal Aboriginality. There is a stunning black and white photograph by Mike Jackson, of Aboriginal traditional dancers in full flight, on the cover of his 1995 *New and Selected Poems*, subtitled Munaldjali, Mutuerjaraera (a tribe of the Beaudesert, Queensland area of Queensland, and "Murri fighter"). Many of his poems from his six collections have Aboriginal dialect titles, use Aboriginal words throughout, and increasingly work with a developing, experimental form of language which seeks to reflect Aboriginal spoken language, and to resist the hegemony of English. In Fogarty's work, the rawness of existence as an Aboriginal in a racist society has taken an extreme linguistic turn. While the subject matter – poverty, loss of identity with the land, systemic and personal violence, race hatreds, loss of oral traditions and language – is necessarily common to so many Aboriginal poets, Lionel Fogarty's poetry has been finding a dramatic new way through the labyrinth of race relations. Grieving the loss of tribal traditions, languages and existence, Fogarty's poetry is attempting to write a spoken Aboriginal tongue which is neither pidgin English nor another, imported kind of postcolonial dialect – say Jamaican English, or black American. His most recent poems broker a space for themselves which is strong, able to accommodate lyricism as well as construct a verbal defiance to the multiple forms of gubba power over Aboriginal people. In his startling new poem, 'Consideration of Black Deaths (story)', he begins:

"No treaty will give us our laws: it can be broken."
Two brothers were killed up here
didn't even have a chance to live
yes they lived short yet long
cos we never forget them
Two sisters up here are dead
by rape and knife cuts
They were drunk with white men
yes it's not all their fault
yes don't blame the white-eyes
It's the societies dat the
rich pigs control.
The sheets and blankets of the cells
are a danger to us
The disposable razor are a danger to us.
Now correctional man in times
you have broken the law

how was it when you didn't know
our custom and cultures
you didn't know my tribe
my people's land needs…

(from New and Selected Poems:
Munaldjali, Mutuerjaraera)

Confrontational, both linguistically and in content, Fogarty's poetry carries both the full weight of ignorance and violence between the races, and a strident call for justice. It's not just a utopian call for a return to Aboriginal traditions and language which his poetry calls for, because the realisation of the complexity of the present is always there in the poetry. But there is a constant linguistic struggle to expose injustice, to rail against the vicious absurdities of white power (see 'Fuck all Departments', 'Ngunda Man Koori', 'Fuck Off' and many other poems), and to instil a pride and presence to Aboriginal languages and a future deeply rooted in historical reality:

Deep down in the black anthropological mind
lives an historical process
you all here never will re-write.
Let's let judging mish-mash encyclopedia
middle primary grades on to your own
distorted conceptions…gubba…migglou..

(from 'Fuck Off')

Fogarty's rage – political, personal, racial – finds a powerful linguistic tool and form in his mixing of dialects, his using up of English against itself, and his strident drive to break up the stereotypes and wisdoms of the gubba and migglou (whites) who preside sanctimoniously over their "re-write" of history. In the orchestrated jumble of his verse he is opening up both a political and aesthetic space for anger, criticism, refusal, new possibilities for the old languages and traditions which are being pen-pushed and legislated against: "Light the burri. / Hear our Koori law. / Departments we destroy" ('Fuck All Departments').

LISA BELLEAR
POSSUM SKIN SPIRIT

Look at my possum skin
cloak.
It cannot be replaced
with your colonising
garments.
I am force fed
repeatedly
bible – bullets – baccy
flour – tea.
Your white chugar
leaves us with a
colonial legacy of legalised
genocide –
diabetes
asthma
cancer
colonial psychosis.
Cloak me with your
whiteness these victorious
Victorian garments.
My spirit will continue

I refuse to be conquered and
post-colonialised.
My story which is yours
tells of strength, survival, and
on going dreams. Come closer,
feel the possum spirit. This can
be our pathway home.

MY MOTHER'S EYES

Sit quietly hear nothing, feel, then search.
I have my mother's eyes, she was your
great great grandmother. All those years
these eyes have waited to be named.
Three generations, here you are, finally
a 'lation.

Feel my eyes, on our mother's
side, you could see the spirit
of the river people. How much
laughter and sadness was witnessed,
through these eyes. My 'lations on
my mother's side, I have waited, we
all have waited.

Feel our mother's eyes, name her,
name all our 'lations. Be
proud.

The Left Hand of Capitalism

JACKET IS A QUARTERLY LITERARY MAGAZINE DISTRIBUTED TO EVERY TOWN, CITY AND
COUNTRY IN THE WORLD VIA THE INTERNET AND GIVEN AWAY FREE. ITS PUBLISHER IS
THE POET JOHN TRANTER. HERE HE MUSES ON THE CONTRADICTIONS OF THE BRAVE
NEW ELECTRONIC WORLD.

I THINK THEY'RE right when they say that middle-aged men shouldn't have children: they're too old to manage the sleepless nights and the effluent disposal problems. But here I am, well over fifty, father to a demanding baby who turned one a few months ago.

The cute little fellow is called *Jacket* magazine, and I'm as proud as any dad. The other day, the counter on the front page ticked over to 30,000.

That tells me that over thirty thousand separate visits have been made to the magazine's Web site on the Internet (http://www.jacket.zip.com.au) since the first issue in October 1997.

This is not quite like having thirty thousand subscribers for a print magazine – a buyer has to buy the magazine, whether they want the whole thing or just one article, whereas a "visit" to *Jacket* might consist of a few minutes worth of browsing, say looking through a few book reviews in Issue # 4, or a whole evening spent reading through a number of issues.

Many of my readers come back often for a regular literary hit; a few land there by accident (scanning the Internet for something smart in dinner jackets, perhaps) and leave immediately, never to return.

There's another difference: magazine subscribers subscribe; that is, they pay money. My readers get *Jacket* for free. Obviously I'll never get rich that way.

But it sure beats trying to edit, print, publish, distribute and sell a print edition of a literary magazine. I've been there, and done that.

In fact I've been involved in editing and publishing poetry books and magazines for over thirty years, on and off. That was in the Age of Print: now, most of what I do ends up on the Internet.

The shift to the Internet is the most significant change that publishing has seen this century. An earlier change, the move from metal type to photo-lithographic printing, was also important, but it wasn't what the trendy pundits call a "paradigm shift"; the Internet is.

The Way We Were: Most of the poetry magazines that were around when I began writing in the early 1960s were printed using metal type and stereo plates on large and costly rotary printing machines weighing a couple of tonnes. In effect we were still in the age of Johannes Gutenberg, who invented moveable metal type over five hundred years ago. The processes were the same: all we had added was a degree of mechanisation.

It is costly to get things done like that. The skills were difficult to obtain, the machinery was expensive. It was also noisy, dirty and dangerous. The Linotype machines that were used to set type for most books and newspapers took a crane to shift them, and the type was cast from vats of poisonous molten metal: a mixture of tin, lead and antimony.

Then in 1961 the IBM Selectric golf-ball typewriter came along, and in 1964 the IBM Magnetic Tape/Selectric Typewriter followed, with a magnetic tape data storage unit. It was small, clean and quiet, and a tenth the price of a Linotype machine, and a competent typist could learn to use it in half a day. Fitted with a carbon-film ribbon and a changeable type-ball that gave a range of typefaces in different sizes from eight to twelve point, it produced razor sharp output that was ideal for use on the new photo-litho offset printing presses that were becoming common.

By the middle of the 1960s small versions of

these presses were appearing in many large offices, replacing the office duplicator. The Multilith 1250 litho press, for example, was inexpensive and relatively compact, and gave high-quality output on foolscap paper. These machines didn't need metal type; they could reproduce anything that you could photograph or photocopy, including drawings, snapshots, a page of typed letters, or a page of handwriting.

So by the second half of the 1960s the equipment for producing an inexpensive poetry magazine was fairly easy to get hold of, and simple to use. This helped to start a flood of little magazines and gave a new generation of young poets a place to be heard, a venue for argument and experimentation, and a shot in the arm.

But it didn't solve the main and the perennial problem of poetry publishing. This is the cost and difficulty of distribution. You can solve all the other problems, but that one is intractable.

Or it was, until the Internet.

Sappho, Callimachus, Catullus, Li Bai and John Donne all had small audiences for their poetry, and any serious poetry faces the same situation today – it's not a profitable market anywhere in the world. Bookshops can only afford to stock popular verse. Canadian bookshops can't afford to stock New Zealand poetry, and vice versa. Few Australian poets are found in the bookstores of Brooklyn; Scottish poets despair of big sales – any sales – in Normal, Illinois.

Enter the Internet: it's relatively cheap, it reaches everywhere there's a telephone line (or a satellite drifting overhead), and it costs the distributor almost nothing. In effect, the purchaser does the work of accessing the material and paying for its delivery.

Here's an example of the reach of the Internet. In the first issue of *Jacket*, I published an interview I had recorded with the British poet Roy Fisher, and received an enthusiastic e-mail from a fan. The fellow was grateful for the chance to read an interview with his favourite poet, he said, and went on to explain: "It's hard to find material on Roy Fisher, up here in Nome, Alaska".

Video and stereo sound are still difficult to send or receive on the Internet because they need a lot of bandwidth, and the telephone lines the Internet uses don't have much bandwidth. We still don't have video-phones, for that reason. But for simple text – poetry, or prose – it's quick, cheap, and ubiquitous.

Some older people find the technology daunting. And it's true that until a few years ago the Internet was hard work. You needed a degree in computer science to get a handle on it. Now, it's easy to browse the Internet. Believe me.

The latest Windows and Macintosh systems, with their graphical interface and easy "click and do it" modus operandi, have made a tremendous difference. The Internet was designed to be cruised by browsers, and current browsers like Netscape (now given away for free) are designed to be logical and easy to use. Most contemporary word processors even come with a built-in program for constructing Internet Web pages. A child can do it; in fact, as most parents know, children are more at home with computers than many adults.

Are there problems? Of course.

For the consumer, the first problem is quality, or rather lack of it. You walk into a good bookshop and go to the poetry section: the books you see have each gone through a process of selection and editorial fine-tuning. Most of them are likely to be of reasonable quality, personal taste aside. But on the Internet, most of the poems you find are awful: uninteresting, unedited, and definitely not fine-tuned.

Anyone can publish anything at all on the Internet, and broadcast it all around the world, without the bothersome interference of censors, style police, or cantankerous editors. Cool!

But as it happens, the bothersome interference of editors is what most readers want. They don't like having to wade through some amateur's first draft. They would much rather read a final draft by a writer who's talented enough to attract the interest of a publisher, and professional enough to listen to an editor's advice.

Then from the other side of the screen, as a magazine editor, how do you find your audience? They're all out there, but where? How do you reach that poetry fan in Nome Alaska and tell him about the Roy Fisher interview, when you don't even know he exists?

You have to depend on word of mouth, mainly, and hope that your magazine is so good that people will hear about it, and look for it using one of the many free search engines, programs that trawl the Web looking for sites that contain a key word or words that you instruct the program to search for.

The third problem is money. The sad fact is that apart from selling pornography, no small organisation can make money on the Internet; not even enough to pay the phone bill. For a magazine to be successful on the Internet, you have to give it away.

What was that, again?

Let me talk about irony for a moment.

Tranter's First Law of Internet Irony has to do with parent/child relationships. Years ago it was common to see parents who couldn't handle the generation gap between themselves and their children. A retired bank manager and his wife, say, decent people with conservative views and a sound superannuation policy, watched in horror as their kids grew their hair long, dropped out of school, smoked dope and indulged in Free Love. Only a few years later (it seems to me) you met their children's children: middle-aged hippies whose long hair was turning grey, and whose kids in turn hated Leonard Cohen, loudly despised their parents for taking drugs, and were ashamed that their house didn't have a dishwasher and an indoor pool.

The Internet's like that. It was set up by US military types with short back-and-sides haircuts to facilitate scientific military research among a string of US universities, and it was cleverly designed to be impervious to damage from Russian nuclear attack or terrorist bombs.

The phone and power systems we depend on are hierarchical: knock out Central Control and the whole thing falls over. Two or three well-placed bombs can render half the telephones in the United States useless. That spells trouble for the US Defense Forces.

The Internet was designed to get around that problem. The electronic messages that throng the Internet are designed to find their own way to their destinations without the help of any Central Control; they route themselves through a loose and adaptable network of interconnected computers choosing whichever phone connection looks the fastest from moment to moment. There is no one in charge. Knock out half the computers and half the phone lines, and things slow down a bit, that's all. As long as there are two or more of you sending messages to each other, the Internet's alive.

This lack of central control meant that as well as the boffins, other people in US universities – long-haired hippies, for example – could set up virtual communities of like minds on the Internet, and exchange recipes for marijuana cookies and terrorist bombs, and no one could stop them.

So a culture of free exchange and mutual help has come into being in cyberspace, an economic model based on the hippy ideal of the barter of intangible goods. If you have a problem understanding a computer program, say, and ask for assistance on the Internet, you'll get a hundred replies, with no strings attached, except that you'll feel an obligation to help others in the same way. As ye give, so shall ye receive. An anthropologist might call it a "gift culture".

Conversely, it's costly and bothersome to set up credit-card payment mechanisms on the Internet. I feel if I asked for payment for *Jacket*, my readers would simply go elsewhere. There's plenty of free stuff out there.

And this leads to Tranter's Second Law of Internet Irony: Weird Things Happen to Capitalism on the Internet. Think of one of those pink rubber kitchen gloves. If you pull a (pink) right-handed kitchen glove inside out, you get a (silver) left-handed glove. That's what the Internet does to capitalism: it pulls it inside out.

In the so-called real world, you have to make sure your revenue is greater than your expenditure; what's left is your profit, and the measure of your success. On the Internet, it's the other way around.

So *Jacket* is free, and thus – sadly – the contributors don't get paid.

At first I thought that very few writers would want to publish in *Jacket* without being paid, but so far that doesn't seem to be a problem. The following are among the many kind souls who have given their work to Jacket for no tangible reward: John Ashbery, Charles Bernstein, Carolyn Burke, Tom Clark, Alfred Corn, Elaine Equi, Roy Fisher, Mark Ford, David Lehman, Harry Mathews, Ron Padgett, Bob Perelman, Marjorie Perloff, Carl Rakosi, John Redmond, Peter Riley, Ron Silliman, Nathaniel Tarn, Shamoon Zamir, and Eliot Weinberger.

But if *Jacket* is free – and it carries no advertising – where do I get the money to do all this?

Let's look back to the days of Gutenberg for a moment.

A conventional literary quarterly usually has about three primary staff (say two editorial and a typist/office assistant), as well as having to pay for the work of a typesetter, layout or pasteup artist, platemaker, printer, binder and warehouse staff. That's say ten people. You need to rent an office. Postage costs are a nightmare. The annual total cost – salaries, expenses, printing costs, postage – has to be minimum US$30,000 up to say a maximum of $100,000. You certainly can't afford to print in colour; that adds another $20,000 a year at least.

Then you find it's almost impossible to get the magazine into New York or London, let alone into say Nome, Alaska.

Jacket has one staff – I'm it, there's no one else – and no office. My own writing desk is the office. The main cost is my time; which means I don't get much poetry written these days.

I pay around $1,000 per year for Internet access and fax and phone and stationery and postage et cetera. Those are my total costs – $1,000 instead of $100,000.

So, it's cheap. But it takes up most of my waking life. Why do I do it?

Jacket is hard work, and I like hard work. I enjoy editing the poems and articles and taking photos of people and designing the pages, and I even enjoy writing the HTML (hypertext markup language) typesetting code that underlies the pages. *Jacket* exercises all my various talents – and it's fun.

It has also enlarged my circle of friends by a factor of about ten. And I feel I've enabled a lot of writers to find a wider international audience for their work, especially younger poets. I received a lot of generous support and assistance when I was a young writer, and it's good to be able to give something back.

After all, despite the best intentions of the US Defense Department, that's what the Internet's all about.

You can find *Jacket* at http://www.jacket.zip.com.au

M. T. C. CRONIN
SPIES

Six unknown named agents appeared to me with paper plots
Of the sea-floor

Asking, *What did you see from the satellite?*
That we have reduced truth down to steam?

On your side of the ocean a bargain was struck
To keep the clock which kept old hours, to laugh
at beggars, to collect antiques and to spit
at stones

Startling and for the record I could only reply candidly
That if there is in fact no excuse
For not doing what you can do
But rather the exact right thing
Then my life until now has been useless
And no amount of surveillance is likely to produce
The clean cut of a line or even the expected
Disobedience of the unavoidable self –

And just like a dream the spies floated away, telling nothing . . .

CHRIS WALLACE-CRABBE
THE DRUNKEN COLOURS

What is the basis for the pleasure you can take
in simply writing down a mistake?
Whatever may be, it's dusty spring,
allergies doing their own sweet thing,
physiology at work on mental states
and pollens reborn in the guise of fates

       Fate, will, decision, ha!
They stick in that blankety darkness
which has cocooned them ever since
the honey of classical antiquity.
Can the water in the stream erode itself?
But if it's right that understanding
leaps from the same idea as substance
could it then be that disaster
               refers to a starless night
when you feel the darkness trampling through your body
and hear Fuselian horses chomping
the crisp grass of summer under stringybarks?

What shall we do with discomfort we take
from finding that most of our feelings are at stake?
Whatever the case, it's autumn now
and clouds float like blouses on the hill's brow
watercolouring my neural state
in humid washes of desire and fate.

TWO POEMS BY PETER BOYLE
GRAVEYARD BY THE SEA
- VARIATIONS ON A POEM BY PAUL VALÉRY

O récompense après une pensée
Qu'un long regard sur le calme des dieux!
Paul Valéry, *Le Cimetière Marin*

(Our reward after all thought is done,
this long gaze into the calm of gods.)

I
Calm rooftop where white doves are gliding
among the pines, among the tombs
it trembles
riddled with fire:
the sea the sea.
Where the sun rests on the ocean's depths
time shimmers its long blue gaze;
white sails skim
the carved curved face of gods.

Surrounded by my seaward glance,
I climb this hill where flametrees twist.
The cicadas' sharp cry grates against dry grass.
Among the white flock of peaceful tombs
all's burnt, unmade, fed back to air.

Like fruit that melts into sensation
trading absence for delight
in the mouth where its form dies
I breathe in here the fine smoke of my future.
Waves thud against the edge of rocks.
At each step climbing the hill
I grow used to what I'm drawing into my lungs:
not salt not foam but time
sharp as dry air
subtle as sun bent by waves.

To walk here among cousins and unknown intimates
to whisper the blue eyes of my grandfather
sifting the nineteen twenties through ears of grass.

Among the roots of trees
the sharp cries of young girls,
their eyes, teeth, moist eyelids,
the blood that shone on lips as they opened,
the last gifts, the fingers that controlled them –
these lives passed on to wilt among the flowers.
Between the void and the pure event,
I listen for whatever echo my fate holds
like someone pressing their ear to a rusted water tank
to catch, reverberating in its depths,
bitter pure black sounds.
Down the long aisles of this stone city
my shadow outpaces me:
thistles in yellow heat,
signatures the spiders scribe
on the rafters of a house.
These once inhabited heads –
the faithful sea is sleeping on my tombs.

II
If I stand on this hill, setting my back to the ocean,
I can look clear across the harbour's tidal run
into my childhood:
the familiar cream wall, a patch of greenness,
the red-tiled roof where strangers live now,
and that thin road that climbs above the beach.
Sunlight caught by waves
reflects from windows of cars descending streets
where my childhood has become
a silent ball that bounces
and does not bounce.

From too much watching, the scene trembles,
starts to slip
just as sometimes at night alone in a house
we become aware how everything is moving:
the house creaking, rearranging itself,
expanding and contracting floorboards,
shedding its skin of paint, its crumbling line of dust,
and we see
how the shelters we make for lovemaking
are also tombs.

I lift my gaze beyond the gravestones:
sea,
eye that seals within itself
so much sleep beneath its veil of fire.
Out there on quiet waves
the sailboats like startled birds
peck the thousand crumbs of light
midday sets rippling in its blue unfolding.

Standing thin and clear
on this hillside poised between two seas:
my childhood harbour and the wider ocean:
out of a difficult idleness, thirty years late,
I have wandered to this place of shining,
grey tombs at midday above a sea
where white boats tack in wind.

My shadow moves slowly
along the houses of the dead:
red mud, bright flowers, what we become.

THE TRANSFORMATION BOAT

Just an old plain boat travelling the coastline
and wherever it came to rest its prow against the wharf
from small town to small town
life suddenly would arrive in people's houses.
Dogs and children would stir around midnight
touched by the light that comes from there,
a wavering across all that darkness.
Thin stars would penetrate the hands of business men
and make them give away all their belongings
and enter into the fire
or a woman would walk out of a house at dawn
and wake next standing in the souk at Marrakesh,
her midriff spangled in gold, dancing in ecstasy,
her twining arms freed to the sky's rapture.

The boat would glide into the harbour at midnight
and sail off before dawn
and in the plaza of the quiet town
a fun girl would be rolling a hoop at sunset

while other children dart in and out of doorways,
sheltering behind bushes and tall mysterious garbage bins,
playing at gangsters and police,
and all the time
the boat's sails grew steadily like a shadow in their minds.

Someone said Odysseus was on board
and if you stood before the skipper's wheel at full noon
you'd see the crew were Circe's swine rooting their noses in swill.
Another said it was the Flying Dutchman,
another the boat to the Fortunate Isles.

In plain day without leaving anywhere
a girl at the sink draining pasta would kneel to receive the lord.
A small wren would speak from the freezer section of the supermarket
and I would take my fear of breakage and walk forward steadily
the way dreams do.

When the boat left someone saw water tumbling out of the sky –
a boy recorded how midsummer snow
was falling across the outback.
And all that blocks us from loving would pass away
like mist over glass
and our hands wiped clean of every line
could begin at last their journey to the sun.

DENNIS HASKELL
WALKING IN ENGLAND, LATE NOVEMBER

History greets the present when
at pedestrians on a three-cobblestone-wide
path trodden angular
by the ceaseless hammering of feet
a truck belches and lurches.
Stone statues discreetly stare, a little
more blackened with every exhaust
under England's drizzling miseries of sky.

Undeterred, Cambridge faces burnt with cold
walk past, cycle past, talk past
this bookshop- and scholar-strewn village

before their bustling retreat
into heat-drunk rooms.

I can find kings who trudged up
here majestically, in the mud;
that lax student, Wordsworth; nature's evocations;
or Milton, late by candlelight
beginning to read himself blind.
The truck's horn stammers,
the Cam is still, its bridge inconsequential,
and the Cambridge traffic
gridlocks again.

Here are the residents exiting shops not
much more than holes in the wall,
their arms weighed down.
What of the present could seem heroic?
Yet here, even those
walking alone do not walk out alone,
monuments and heroes become human,
and the great consequences of history.
A truck belches. Dishwater still,
sky and water move
imperceptibly towards
another Spring.

KEVIN HART
HER KISS

He knew that it was many years ago
    When he first loved her, when he met
Her in a restaurant with someone else, and that
The blurry feeling when he saw her smile
    At work or in a supermarket queue

Meant he had been a tangent to his life.
    He knew all that; but only when,
One day, he heard himself pronounce her name
To someone passing in the corridor,
And was surprised by tenderness,

He understood that it was far too late,
    That old mistakes will multiply

Inside the heart, or cancel themselves out.
But which was it? Well, she was married now
    And surely never thought of him

Like that, then he remembered how she looked
    When someone hugged him in the bar,
How email from her ending "With regards"
Had changed to "Yours". He lived inside her kiss
    Two weeks before the moment came

And three days after. When she turned to him,
    And he could see the downy hairs
Above her lips, his hands reached round her back,
And all her fascination was condensed
    Into a kiss that neither felt

Till later in their separated homes:
    When putting children down to sleep,
When lying with the darkness all around,
He touched again the ridges of her spine,
    She knew the hungers of his mouth.

JOHN TRANTER
GROVER LEACH

"Goodbye, old teacher .... Goodbye, Old Dog Tray."
    John Ashbery, 'And You Know'

I

It's Saturday, meet me tonight,
Grover said to a young lady at the State Fair –
meet me under the electric light
that burns in the sky over the hot dog stand
under the Ferris Wheel by the edge of the bay.
Let the farm slumber in the night-air,
let the corn nod under the spray
as the waves beat against the land.
Meet me where the mob's roar
drowns our laughter, and our mad fling
will magnetically excite each strand
of feeling in the crowd, and the Wheel will begin
to spin and spark like a dynamo, and bring
the wonderful twentieth century rolling in!

II

I remember long ago
the ocean regularly brought
to the bay an ancient tidal flow,
and fish were caught, that's what we
sought, as kids, and thought
about the 'Old Dog Tray' and the sea –
a tea tray painted in simple faith
with a picture of a dog on the shore,
his bushy tail furled
and his ears pricked to hear
beyond the waters' roar
a drowning farmer's breath.
For Grover, life on the farm had grown drear
and he learned to despise the modern world.
His wife left him, though his heart was true,
the farm failed, and that's why, it seems
old Grover waded in, and drowned his dreams.
And so the farm sleeps, waiting for a new
owner, and Rover waits too in that yellow light
that seems to paint the wet sand with pain
so it resembles a watery plain
where screaming seabirds dash their reflected flight
over the glitter of the State Fair, Saturday night.

'Grover Leach' uses the end words of Matthew Arnold's 'Dover Beach'.

THOMAS SHAPCOTT
THE OLD WINDOW

His architect had played the post-modern game –
allusions everywhere but never serious,
illusions short-sheeted, as in the classic maze
(one-quarter size) that set off the Rotunda
(pure Raj, that) where the outdoor drinks'
casquet was the Party Piece. That first summer
he used the Orangerie the once,
for the Corporate Retreat (the name fooled nobody);
it was a pure assertion of his trendy nonchalance.
Later he hired out the space for wedding groups
(his maze was trampled by Mediterranean types).
The ground floor area also was public as an Insurance lobby
or the Piazza of one of the Accountancy agglomerates.

The Grand Staircase, a cheeky salute to the TITANIC,
invited theatrical gestures, and it got them.
Nobody would forget Amanda abandoning her seven veils
as she ascended to the upstairs bathroom
and her nip of Mothers Downfall. Or Genevieve
breasting the bannister in the altogether
too degagé mink stole. He had his parties,
everyone remembered. It was a fun place,
Raouls Verseilles. There was an attic
or at least a Mansard roof and small rooms.
Each small window was different (that was the trick)
and he had insisted to the architect
that the furthest window must be the genuine thing,
a tiny multi-paned dormer ripped
from the chateau his grandmother once haunted
outside Lyons. It was only in the wettest day of winter
that he finally clambered up and regarded the memento.
Perhaps it had been enough to know it was there.
He had looked at it in Australia once before, out of storage,
and the slap of antipodean light, brash as an appraising squint
over the tanned bodies in Bondi out to the glittering surf
had reduced that sheltered window frame to an imperfect excuse
for clumsy glass and bubbly surfaces (which he once remembered
as meaningful). He saw through it, it might be said.
But in winter glumness, with drops clustering
like dismal starlings on the outer panes, he re-entered its world.
He had not escaped after all.
His mother still trembled for him, and remained as powerless.
His father slammed the door again and the same pane cracked.
His grandmother was as imperious and demanded her price.
And he was the still-young boy again. "Mon petit serviteur",
she had said, again and again, "Serviteur"
as she instructed him, cruelly, in all the arts.
The Mansard attic was his choice. Even then
he only had to raise one finger and he knew she was lost.
So he came home to this, because loss is power
and power is lost, and because illusion
can be allusion, after all, in the end.

TWO POEMS BY JOHN KINSELLA
AFTER SIR LAWRENCE ALMA-TADEMA'S
'94° IN THE SHADE' (1876)

for Peter Porter

"THYRSIS:
Sit down now, goatherd, (think the Nymphs had asked you)
And play your pipe, here where the hillside steepens
And tamarisks grow on the slope. I will watch your goats."
                              Theocritus, *Idyll* 1

The country in summer. The temperature hovers
        around the low thirties –
it is something of a heat wave. The surrounding
fields are tawny gold, though green tinges are almost
        tactless within a world
contracted to the killing jar. Unseen birds fuse,
tarnish with a chemical sky. Sullen trees wreck

the view so it's photosensitive. Animals
        twitch beneath the herbage.
Landscape and portrait hang languidly about each
other. In the foreground a youth is spread out cheek-
        in-hand, reading a book
on butterflies. His weapon – the butterfly net –
lies in front of him. He is confident. Maybe

overconfident. He's wearing an ivory
        summer suit with "pith hat";
schoolboy on holidays, resting in the still shade,
confident within the granary of empire, wealth
        that keeps home secure.
Butterflies from other spaces congregate. Stooks
have been gathered, but lie in casual disarray.

HOCKNEY'S DOLL BOY AT THE LOCAL COUNTRY WOMEN'S ASSOCIATION ANNUAL MUSICAL: WHEATBELT, WESTERN AUSTRALIA

Opening night. As the curtain lifts
Doll Boy hovers in the wings
the Town Hall full as the star drifts

centre-stage and in a falsetto sings
to the roar of the crowd –
the CWA already counting the takings

as the chorus of footy stars makes a loud
entry – smeared make-up and wigs,
ill-fitting blouses, the odd shroud-

length dress. A farmer digs
a mate in the ribs – that strapping
girl's my son, the last vestiges

of his reserve dissipating
with the electricity of the occasion.
At interval, the cast is buzzing

with excitement, taking slices of melon
from Doll Boy's chipped green plate,
blowing him kisses, calling him "Queen".

You're just not cute enough to rate
a place among us! Doll Boy, eyes
to himself, begins to create

a space apart, beyond the cries
of the crowd, the taste of melon on his lips:
pink crystals bristling like stars,

full and sweet. And he grips
the memory of the vine – intricately
binding the patch near the roses and strips

of everlastings, ripening rapidly,
drinking the dam's muddy water insatiably,
preparing to feed the elect, delicately.

THE CLASSIC POEM

1. SELECTED BY THE EDITORS

'AT COOLOOLAH' CAN be seen as a keynote poem for this issue – a sombre reflection on Australia's central dilemma.

JUDITH WRIGHT

AT COOLOOLAH

The blue crane fishing in Cooloolah's twilight
has fished there longer than our centuries.
He is the certain heir of lake and evening,
and he will wear their colour till he dies,

but I'm a stranger, come of a conquering people.
I cannot share his calm, who watch his lake,
being unloved by all my eyes delight in,
and made uneasy, for an old murder's sake.

Those dark-skinned people who once named Cooloolah
knew that no land is lost or won by wars,
for earth is spirit: the invader's feet will tangle
in nets there and his blood be thinned by fears.

Riding at noon and ninety years ago,
my grandfather was beckoned by a ghost –
a black accoutred warrior armed for fighting,
who sank into bare plain, as now into time past.

White shores of sand, plumed reeds and paperbark,
clear heavenly levels frequented by crane and swan –
I know that we are justified only by love,
but oppressed by arrogant guilt, have room for none.

And walking on clean sand among the prints
of bird and animal, I am challenged by a driftwood spear
thrust from the water; and, like my grandfather,
must quiet a heart accused by its own fear.

Reproduced by permission of Carcanet Press from *Collected Poems.*

Women Making Our World

JUDITH RODRIGUEZ ON JUDITH WRIGHT AND GWEN HARWOOD

THIS WEEKEND, THE *Herald Sun* published a supplement entitled 'Australian of the Century'. They're not giving the remaining twenty-one months a chance to revise the choices of thirty-five nationally prominent figures asked to name their "greats". The worthy winner, by the way, is Howard Florey, the developer not of piles of bricks, but of penicillin. No writer makes the top ten, unless you count the writings of Florey, Bradman, Weary Dunlop and Nugget Coombs. Rupert Murdoch, who reneged on publishing a writer under contract, comes in eighth (in his own paper).

Of literary figures, Patrick White rates six nominations; Germaine Greer two, Joseph Furphy and Catherine Helen Spence one each. Henry Lawson gets two – this must be his nadir; perhaps the line of the century, dividing his published works, handicapped him? Other poets taken for a run are Banjo Paterson (7, with one nomination to head the list!), Barry Humphries (2) and Mary Gilmore and Judith Wright (1 each).

Judith Wright, as the sole living poet mentioned (Humphries might acknowledge his poems, many in his stage-voices, as a *violon d'Ingres*) receives a strangely reductive note on her life achievement.

> Poet. Her first collection... explored her relationship with her "blood's country". She contined to write often lyric verse about the country, and denounce the tide of progress. She was an early environmentalist...She neglected her poetry in the 1970s, joining campaigns for Aboriginal rights and 'We Call For a Treaty' in 1985. The boundaries between her poetry and her activism have blurred. Some critics call her shrill; others the conscience of the nation.

What a policing of the poet! Who can only be understood to have one topic, or one and a half. Who must not neglect her poetry, though others are praised for having several busy careers, or preoccupations. Activism, argument, polemic are deplorable unless time has made the poet's convictions comfortably commonplace. Of course, the assumptions of the readers of the *Herald Sun* are summed up in the description of the subject of Wright's activism as "the tide of progress".

Harwood and Wright occupy that interesting interval – I almost wrote "interregnum" – where the poet's silence, through untimely death (for Harwood was writing with no diminution of finesse and spirit, in her seventies) or tiredness or deflection of energies, allows a public decision of sorts to be made. Perhaps it is the space for critics and scholars to assemble the papers and their points before they feast upon the corpus! It may be a kind of "wait-and-see": when we open our open our eyes again, will the poet be still with us?

Wright's has been a pervasive presence, frequently inconvenient to the critics as it changed shape. I was too young to receive her first book, *The Moving Image* (1946), which coming immediately after the war set a reconciliation course for Australian poetry. Modernism had received its comeuppance; but for Wright the issues were elsewhere, with the land and its lovers, both black and white. There was plenty here that suggested the bush muse, so that half-caste Josie, returned soldier-farmers and the ancient rumours of massacred Aborigines could be accepted along with a Mosaic interpretation of 'Bullocky'; and there were lyrics of love, so that the ancient ceremonies of the bora ring and the ghostly claim of the dispossessed elder could find words in an emotional realm to which readers held clues.

In her next book Wright pleased the benign academics by a bracket of particularly "womanly" poems: "Woman's song", "Woman to child", "Woman to man"...ending "the blaze of light along the blade. / Oh hold me, for I am afraid". She also articulated her vision of life in "The Cycads", and (less noticed) her vision of pain, the "time-bomb world":

> Pain, what is it? That which keeps alive
> amoebae doubling from the acid...hedge of swords
> beside the road from protoplasm to man...
> Manjack home from the wars walked down the
> street,
> and in his flesh a fire that ate him lean.
>
> ('Pain')

The critics who responded to her vulnerability were not so pleased when she sat down to think of the mythic shapes behind vulnerable life, of the world as Heracleitian fire "with measures of it kindling, and measures going out." In 1957, Vincent Buckley writing in *Meanjin* deplored what he saw as a philosophical, false direction – for a woman. Premonitions of the world's end were not the official version, not the optimism demanded by the 'fifties and still hankered after in the 'sixties.

For some reason Wright's admirers faltered when her latest book was simply – *Birds*. Yesterday I heard a lecturer refer to the bird as symbol for the poem. Certainly the Parliaments of Fowles have shown them as speaking with human voices. And when I came to make my private anthology of Wright, I found there too poems that spoke for a change in me, a change in everything.

This anthology is the heart of what I have to say about these poets, parents in practice to many poets in Australia and (going by the devotion expressed by some very young writers) casting longer shadows than most.

The middle 'seventies were, in Australia, a feminist ferment and I cannot have been the only reader of poetry who evinced dissatisfaction with the poems they'd been "taught", by making a new list, a list which obeyed Wright's own prohibition by eschewing the overused 'Bullocky'. It included 'For Precision', 'Gum-trees Stripping', 'Double Image', 'To Hafiz of Shiraz'...but most feelingly 'Ishtar', 'Dove-Love', 'Eve to her Daughters' (irritable and all), 'Remembering an Aunt', 'Naked Girl and Mirror' and 'Heloise Wakening'. (You can see I was using the 1971 *Collected Poems*). The key poem, to me, was 'Naked Girl and Mirror'. At its simplest, with the voice of a goddess it claims the primacy of the self unsubmitted to the carnal program; but it also claims the dignity of amibivalence as a pattern for understanding oneself.

> I may miss your going, some day,
>   though I shall always resent your dumb and fruitful
>   years.
> Yours lovers shall learn better, and bitterly too,
>   if their arrogance dares to think I am part of you.

Wright's 'Heloise' is a more complex refusal to be the prey of a program – to pretend to find whole-

> [Harwood] is a wit, a full-on sophisticate with the range from gentle to majestic, with metaphorical applications from the strict allegory to jeering fantasy. Wright's humour seems to me less "useful", less a stop to be manipulated in the total harmony...

ness in a remnant capacity for life.

This is where, for me, Harwood came in. Her own 'Bullocky' – the work that for too many defines and limits an appreciation of her writing – may for the young be 'Barn Owl', and for my second Wrightian self must be the two sonnets 'In the Park' and 'Suburban Sonnet'. Yet their precision and wit, the tone – elegiac or mock-elegiac? – live in her other modes and other models: her lives of Eisenbart and Krote, her meditations on music, painting, philosophy and their makers, her games-playing with lust that becomes a long meditation on mind and body. Re-reading, I find her subjects cross elsewhere with Wright's: her 'Oyster Cove', for instance, is darker than almost anything Wright wrote of Australia's genocide.

But – it is a large "but": Harwood read much, and her reading entered her fully; and she is a wit, a full-on sophisticate with the range from gentle to majestic, with metaphorical applications from the strict allegory to jeering fantasy. Wright's humour seems to me less "useful", less a stop to be manipulated in the total harmony; at its most obvious in the period sketch of mother and children by the waterfall in 'Request to a Year' and the irritable, domestic plain-speaking of 'Even to Her Daughters'. Perhaps this is to say that Wright is a less various "self" at the heart of her poems.

I turn to late poems by Wright and Harwood. Wright's *Phantom Dwelling* (1985) has one extraordinary poem, which I add to my private Wright canon: 'Smalltown Dance', on the folding of sheets, a universal ceremony also written of by Rosemary Dobson. But 'The Shadow of Fire (Ghazals)' is a remarkable group, dense, questioning, thoughtful. They return to many of her themes, and tantalisingly mention a new interest in Japanese traditions. I cannot dismiss these as merely late or slight.

The Present Tense does a great kindness to those who admired Gwen Harwood's extraordinary, off-by-heart performances of her own occasional verse. As a final section the book prints her 'Syntax of the Mind: on receiving an honorary Doctorate of Letters from the University of Tasmania, April 16, 1988' and Tasmanian Peace Trust 1993 Lecture. They set a high mark for such self-imposed virtuosities.

No less precious are the anecdotes and stories, which leads me to what may well become the best-known of Australian memoirs-in-letters: *Blessed City: Letters to Thomas Riddell 1943*. This is Brisbane in a vital moment of its growing: a backwater suddenly become home to the War Front and the invading Yanks, but before the high-rise. It is also Gwen Foster, whose qualities of mind are prodigally displayed as jokes, sketches, comments, records of the time and place, with high spirits enough to fuel any ordinary city's energy needs for a century. What keeps all this cleverness and bounce from being "mere" anything? It's permeated with the love of all of curious creation, and the glow of joy in a beloved city: perhaps Gwen Harwood's best poem.

Judith Wright's prose output over the years has depressed some of those who saw her poetic output slow. Her conscience moved her from the literary essays of *Preoccupations in Australian Poetry* (a fine, field-defining work amidst the dither of third-class critics) to the essays which outlined her humanitarian, edeucational

Judith Wright

and ecological concerns in *Because I Was Invited, We Called for a Treaty*, and *Going on Talking*. Wright was appalled at the way poems were "taught", and at the way in which "Australianness" was claimed. She told us that even generations of family land-holding in the Dawson River valley and New England, did not give her the depth of belonging and understanding that indigenous Australians possessed. Once I met her in the catalogue room of the National Library, busily researching the dark other side of her family history, *Generations of Men*. This was to become *The Cry for the Dead*, about the pattern of dispossession and genocide in the Dawson Valley in Central Queensland.

In another vein, in a speech to A.U.L.L.A., she told women what it had meant that the land in her family was automatically placed in the legal possession of male heirs only. Most of her writing life, Wright made a living as a chicken farmer. Indignant

at the small earnings from writing poetry, she often sold her poetry by the page and cared tremendously about the copyright the schools and universities blithely ignored. About a year ago, she attended a protest meeting about Public Lending Right; she could not walk unaided but, in the cause, allowed herself to be chivvied by a pack of photographers into "photo-worthy" positions on a stairwell.

Her latest book is a little book of the stories about "when you were little", the stories that don't always have a high point, that include being questioned and go back over the bits that matter – personally. *Tales of a Great Aunt: A Memoir* has a lot more to say about living in the country, and dogs and horses (and the falls that did Wright extensive damage), than about human beings; about brothers and aunts, than about her parents. Except that when you read carefully, her father is a given; and the first chapter makes clear to me for the first time the importance of her mother's illness and early death, from the after-effects of 'flu in the great epidemic. This little book is a precious gift of insights into a life made independent and lonely and thoughtful, a life of stature in which the mode of utterance is secondary to what must be said. We are fortunate that, like Oogeroo, Wright found poetry and what must be said, together.

Harwood might be called urbane; yet her passion is less reticent and more personal than Wright's. She exemplifies the nuanced riches of a cultivated intelligence; she is admirable for her technical skill; in many moods, from the grave to the flip, her distinctive voice holds us spell-bound. Yet Wright's extended development – if you like, a long "making up her mind"; less satiric than Harwood, and less the poet of many voices – now seems almost to record, as it in fact goaded into being, some changes of the Australian heart. Both these poets are dear to me, but Wright's work is somehow inextricable from what I am – what we are? – today. This is a quality we seek, and when we find it it is often called greatness.

ANDREW TAYLOR

FROM: SUITE IN THE OLD STYLE

II THE VISITOR

A single codger with a rickety gait
knocked at my door, demanding bed and food.
I told him his request had come too late
business was closed, his voucher was no good
furthermore this was a private house
not some charity hostel such as he
might feasibly seek out. (This year
winter is chasing even the poorest mouse
out of its church in search of private support.)

He fixed me with the blank unfocussed glare
of the very old, although his age was not
easy or even possible to guess.
"I was here", he wheezed, "before the grass
your father used to mow was even set,
before the trench was dug where the first row
of stones began the footing of this house
which is big, and surely must have room
somewhere out at the back where I can doss".

"This house is one hundred and ten years old",
I told him, preparing to shut the door.
He laughed. "So what? I won't impose forever.
Just a room at the back, hot water now and then
for a cup of tea or soup. You'll never know
I'm here, you'll never even know
when I leave, since you and I when we go
years hence, we'll go together".
Something about him warmed me to his laughter.

The World that Waited (and goes on waiting)

GLEN PHILLIPS ON AUSTRALIAN LANDSCAPE AND THE ANTI-PASTORAL

STRANGE AS IT may seem, Australian artists – painters, composers, poets and many others, have displayed a fascination with landscapes. And generations of Australian poets also have resolutely devoted themselves to recording the slightest glimpse of anything in their country not quite flattened down. If this took the human form of "unique" Australian characters such as the bushranger, lost explorer, sheep drover or bullock driver, they were still set in the vast and mostly featureless outback. At least it kept the land in its place, as a convenient background for Australia's capital cities of the member states! Here the vast majority of Australians, those "monotonous tribes" of A. D. Hope's well-known poem, "Australia", have traditionally found convenient and more or less comfortable shelter. It wasn't always like this. Watkin Tench, in his 1789-93 *Narrative of the Expeditions to Botany Bay and Account of the Settlement at Port Jackson* shows no hint of these poetic preoccupations with landscape.

Admittedly, he may not have cared for landscapes on the whole, referring as he does to "that sickly autumnal tint which marks English trees". But awareness of the landscape must have developed, since, by 1823, W.C. Wentworth was able to win a British poetry prize with his "Australasia" ode, invoking

those far blue hills,
That pour their thousand swift pellucid rills,
Where Warragamba's rage has rent in twain
Opposing mountains, thund'ring to the plain?
(*A Book of Australian and New Zealand Verse*,
W. Murdoch and A. Mulgan [eds], 1950)

Living on the edge of a landmass, particularly on its western margin can be both intimidating and isolating. This drives you to compensate a fair bit of the time. I was born in Western Australia in the semi-desert Yilgarn region, notable for some of the world's greatest goldmines. No doubt most people have heard of Kalgoorlie, fewer are aware of the existence of Southern Cross. These towns were established by massive gold-rushes last century when the

rich minerals exposed in this most weathered down of continents were finally discovered by the British colonist-invaders. The ancient Gondwanaland massif had long been gnawed down by pre-historic glaciers and subsequent water and wind erosion to form the flattest of all continents. Forty years after my birth I finally saw the European Alps at first hand. Like the Romantic writers from Britain tramping through these mountains at the end of the eighteenth century, I was discovering grandeur in landscape.

It seems that anything like a blue shadow on the horizon was powerfully mystic, evocative to the flatlander Australians. When I was at school, Australian universities were not in the habit of including Australian poetry in the syllabus. But at our government elementary school in my ancient "Reading Book" were a sprinkling of pieces by Australian authors. Here, among the scenes of London's little crossing sweepers and the daffodilly English woods I found a poem which our teacher had skipped. It was called 'Over the Moonbi Ranges' and there in the illustration at last was a recognisably Australian landscape, complete with the blue of the ranges on the horizon. Nowadays, the John Kinsellas, Anthony Lawrences, Caroline Caddys and Andrew Lansdowns, all of whom write considerable numbers of Australian landscape poems, provide a welcome reterritorialising of these sites.

Over two hundred years have passed since Watkin Tench wrote his *Narrative*, and we are nearing the end of the twentieth century. But what stage has Australian poetry reached in its coming to terms with its Australian landscapes? Well, in fact there has been a detectable "clearing of the pasture springs", with some younger Australian poets turning back to rural landscapes. These outback settings were rather neglected for several decades, since about 1968, while most writers in Australia's metropolitan population centres rightly sought to reflect the nation's pre-occupations with urban realities: these familiar to consumer-oriented societies. The world's global village has increasingly become a global city, with more and more features (both positive and negative) being shared between Los

Angeles and Rome, Boston and Beijing, Singapore and Sydney. Now, three decades later, what was considered even revolutionary and at least novel in urban Australian poetry (as compared to the idealised outback of Kendall, Paterson and even the Jindyworobaks like Roland Robinson, Ingamells and Mudie) has perhaps achieved a stasis. Contemporary writing has cast this overwhelmingly familiar urban setting (for most Australians) into a right relation with our worldly pre-occupations. And for this we must thank Dransfield, Tipping, Tranter, Ryan, Walwicz, Sykes, Lansdown, and a host of others.

Fay Zwicky has said in an essay, 'Gallic Sanction: Another look at Brennan', "As far as Australia is concerned, the facts are that Brennan had ideas and standards and brought a welcome professionalism to the literary scene". Nearly one hundred years after Brennan, in this last decade or two, contemporary poets, including the above-mentioned, have made such professionalism a remarkably consistent feature of poetic works performed and published in Australia. Previously, a few poets stood out, some like Brennan and Kenneth Slessor reflecting the complex city-scapes of Sydney, others, like Judith Wright and Randolph Stow, apparently pre-occupied with a de-romanticised rural Australia. Perhaps the more general professionalism today has something to do with national maturity. Richard Rossiter put forward an interesting argument to the 1997 ASAL Conference on 'Land and Identity'. He proposed that there is a process of paradigmatical shifts in the way succeeding generations of authors engage with landscape. He sees the use of "nature" to talk explicitly about the "self" as a kind of progress – from the crudity of the pathetic fallacy to seeing "nature as a shaping force separate from, and beyond the control of, the imagination or language". Thus, faced with a "new" landscape, hitherto not an integral part of the literary heritage of that culture, the writers first begin to adapt vocabulary, adopting some terminology of the indigenous peoples, then embracing aspects of the thought systems which indigenous culture has evolved. These are a people who have co-existed with these landscapes for millennia. David Malouf also has had some interesting comments to make

about how language acquisition is an integral part of "knowing" a landscape. According to Rossiter, however, this hybrid process progresses over time, and through the work of a succession of authors, to the point where:

> Nature is no longer represented as an Other – that-which-I-am-not and nor is it an 'objective correlative' of a true-self – but it becomes 'that-which-I-am'.

In other words, a poet who can combine his or her own personal experience working in a particular landscape with a literary and social inheritance of cultural adjustment and interaction with indigenous culture, creates a poem that is written from within, as if part of, that landscape.

Are there such prodigies amongst contemporary Australian poets? While not simply wanting to draw up lists, I do need to mention some of the writers who seem to me to be reaching or have reached that final stage of identification with the land which Rossiter himself perceives in the work of prose writers such as Winton and Carey. Anthony Lawrence, with each successive collection, and following his experiences of living in New South Wales, Western Australia and Tasmania, transmutes his known landscapes into the potters' clay of his poetry:

> Out from a circle of treeless hills
> I follow the tracks of thirsty animals
> to stand in terracotta light
>   by the Murchison River.
> A feral goat throws a backward glance
> over its horns.
> The glance returned,
> it clicks away on a ridge of shale.
>
> Entering a swamp with flowering parasites
> mistletoe and scarlet runner
> like banners
> of congealing blood folding over my arms -
> I hear waves
> and the serious work of the gulls.
>   (from 'Wildflowers, Tallering Station',
>   *The Viewfinder*)

...a poet who can combine his or her own experience working in a particular landscape with an inheritance of adjustment and interaction with indigenous culture, creates a poem that is written from within, as if part of, that landscape.

Andrew Taylor has, in recent works such as *Sandstone* (University of Queensland Press, 1995), produced a body of poetry largely about Australian landscapes (or seascapes in this case) which makes the self-consciousness that characterised early Australian landscape poetry seem now as if it must have belonged to a separate culture:

Or why so many thousand
unswimmable kilometres of water start
at my feet. Living on an island
no matter how big, reminds me
of edges. The coast is our skin
and what goes on inside it goes on
within. If we climb mountains
swim across lakes, walk the Nullarbor
or tackle the blunt indifference of strangers
we encounter a coast. But what is within
remains there, and we know that only
intermittently, like prints on sand
like weather, like parents. Like
childhood with its crumbled caves, its secret
beaches. Like our deaths. Like our lives.

Caroline Caddy's poems also seem to me to succeed out of a hybridity of identification and detachment which offers an easeful engagement with rural Australian landscapes in which she has lived for many years. And yet, like Taylor and Lawrence, she has considerable experience of other continents – Antarctica to China. Maybe it is helpful to get a perspective on your own land by disengaging with it in voluntary exile, from time to time:

At the brink of this dreaming
with its smells
            of limestone and oil
– which is also the smell
of temples –
I stop by the last of the watertanks
            spaced like stars
                  across the desert
– volumes for thirsty travellers
my car
is one!

                  (from 'Motor Car Dreaming',
                        Working Temple)

I would have liked to comment on the extraordinary developments in contemporary poems by Australian Indigenous authors, but I understand that others are undertaking this project. It is important, however, to recognise that the non-Indigenous poets I have just mentioned above could hardly fail to acknowledge a welcome influence (by example) in the work of Oodgeroo Noonuccal (Kath Walker), Jack Davis, Lionel Fogarty, Bobbi Sykes and Mudrooroo.

Some years ago I assisted in the final preparation of an anthology of "Australian Lyrical Poetry" for a university in China. Interestingly, many of the choices made by the editors were poets of the Australian landscape, including John Shaw Neilson, Kenneth Slessor, William Hart-Smith, David Campbell, Douglas Stewart, Judith Wright and Dorothy Hewett. And it occurred to me that, although some readers today may categorise their work merely as belonging to Australia's earlier colonial pre-occupations with rural landscapes, there are in such poems the enduring qualities coming from acute observation, crafted reflectively, especially in the images they provide of those landscapes modified by our European settlement. In particular, Hewett's *Collected Poems* (Fremantle Arts Centre Press, 1995) reminds us that her ten volumes of poetry, spanning 55 years, provide a record of the evolution of Australian landscape poetry through to the present day. For she is still writing and publishing! I was brought up in the same wheatbelt farming districts in Western Australia where she was raised and, from the 'Recent Poems' section of this volume, select 'The Brothers'. For me it reinforces her rightful place with the best (and latest) Australian neo-pastoral (or anti-pastoral) poets:

Those ghostly brothers that I never had
larger than life stalking the countryside
their spittle darkening the dust
ungainly men who never married
clodhopping through barbed fences
looping furrows   their shorn ewes
bleating in a ring of crows
the film of ice cracks on the handbasin
the dough rises in a drone of flies.
I meet them in the paddocks in the evening
standing like fence posts in a line of sorrow
they never speak but weather in the glow
a band of light edging the earth's curve.

Although in the 1930s and '40s the Jindyworobaks led by Rex Ingamells, tried strenuously to insert an Australian landscape vocabulary (paying certain respects to central Australian Aboriginal culture) into Australian poetry, their theoretical articulations could best be described as tentative.

I find Les Murray's much more recent analogy of the Athenians and the Boeotians a useful index to the progress of a newer Australian comprehension of why Australians continue to like contemplating the rural from their preferred domicile within an urban environment. In *A Working Forest* there is an essay entitled 'On Sitting back and Thinking about Porter's Boeotia'. Murray's re-categorization of the age-old town-mouse vs country-mouse dilemma is now very well known to Australian poetry readers and often the opposing camps are drawn into battle lines.

Ultimately, I think, it is more important to read Murray's poems themselves to see how brilliantly the polemic of the vernacular republic, as an embodiment of the "Boeotian" tradition, is transmuted within the poem into artefact, becoming an extension of landscape, rather than remaining outside it, in the sense of a commentary.

Brush and orchard forelands stop sheer
with stencilled hands under mossed cliff eaves
and buried rain peeing far down off balconies
stains ink-dark and slows into leaves.

Blued biscuit towers, propped mile-high in screes
of petrified surf. Spear-carrying trees
crowd up there round lintels rolled from caves
above cornstalk farms with iron-hooped graves.

Bleached rusting country, where waterfalls
reanimate froth and stripped-out cars
in hills being cleft by shopping malls.
If sex and help never dawned on Mars

maybe they're unique, and yet to spread
and Sun and Moon and barren stars
revolve round the scrub Earth after all,
pale handprints climbing an old smoked wall.

('Sandstone Country')

It seems fitting to turn to one of the younger Australian poets closely identified with landscape, John Kinsella. He has merged experimental work (as in the *Syszgy* collection) with the depiction of outback Australian "places". Very frequently the locus is the "wheatlands", his family's farms, such as I know well myself in the Avon Valley district of Western Australia. What readers have found arresting in Kinsella's work is that it challenges any notion of the rural as an idyllic environment. In a recent interview with Brian Henry (published in *Verse*) he ironically warned that there is

not much for the city folk to learn from the simple, pure and spiritual ways of the country. Pastoral as urban moral guidance construct starts to look a little leaky.

Kinsella's own poetry should be the exemplar of his anti-pastoral mode, at one with the "subversive and admirable brethren" of Randolph Stow in the latter's laceration of Australia's settler/invaders in 'The Utopia of Lord Mayor Howard'. Kinsella's *The Hunt*, his eighth volume of poetry, contains the following intentionally anti-pastoralist (appropriately irregular) sonnet:

That the Theocritan ute has been versed
in country things seems obvious, the velour
on the dashboard crazy with fresh air
rushing through the doorless cabin, the cursed
skies blackened by night. Though a moon lurks
somewhere and the spotlight cutting through
the burn-back of summer detects the jerks
of nerves and tissue – the rabbits out to chew
the burnt prongs of stubble, the halogen's
conglomeration filling the omni-screens
within their eyeballs – the crack and whine
of a triple two mocks its rituals, a sign
of fading influence in a field where gravity
is a neck chop and the poem is framed by levity.

('The Rabbiters: A Pastoral')

In a couple of thousand words it isn't possible to survey even one sector of contemporary Australian poetry. From my comparative isolation (Perth to the nearest capital city is the distance from Madrid to Moscow) in this western part of the Australian continent, one does tend to notice the significant contribution of major Australian poets from this region – many, such as Philip Salom, Tracy Ryan, Wendy Jenkins, Alan Alexander, Alec Choate, Hal Colebatch, Nicholas Hasluck, Kenneth MacKenzie, Dennis Haskell and Lee Knowles, would head an impressive list, with a number of books to their credit. Equally, a list of major figures in contemporary Australian landscape poetry from all the other states of Australia would fill pages.

What I have tried to show, from the less

commonly presented West Australian viewpoint, is that landscape as subject for poetry in this country began with the apparent serious disadvantage of a not-very-picturesque country! No lake district or equivalent to the European Alps, the Rockies, none of the world's great rivers (with the possible exception of the Murray), nor the rich archeology of Mediterranean culture, lie "out there". However, a progress can be seen, I believe, in the validity of contemporary Australian poets' engagement with landscape. This literature has only had about two-hundred years of existence, despite the enormous resource of indigenous culture available to the settler/invader writers. Landscape as "outback", "city" or "surf and sea" looks as if it will remain a pre-occupation here for a few more centuries. Despite an "unpromising" physiography, the waiting land has revealed its subtleties and secrets, especially insights provided by the "conquered" indigenous inhabitants, who waited forty millennia or more for us, the imperfect articulators which we Australian poets have proved to be!

LEITH MORTON

THE TWENTIETH CENTURY: A RUMBA

I

Teeth in shoals of shameful gluttony fasten upon the
hideous spectacle of Kitchener abrading crabs & mud
from his spiny sharkskin boots; moths erupt
in an oven of white noise from knots of cotton-weed.
Foch arches his gums & mouths a hopeless hymn: forcing
fists through flesh vents fistulae of violence comparable only
to the parable of scarified artifice (which we recognise by
a certain damp efflorescence). War-wounds weep. A 1918
juggernaut.

II

A hot wave of fever. Blind to reason & ignorant of
our historical caress of the agricultural carreza Göring
invokes a functional unction: the metaphor of Nazism as Neo-
Gothic excess (a singularly ugly proposal): a wine-dark stain
spreading on the pavement. Into the red light projected by
the downpouring of Trotsky's blood floats a gull's curlew, loose
over the winter surf.

III

Biblical satire may sate the natives but few
cannibalize insignificant flesh. Thus the parable
of burnt lamb.
The elite were persuaded to elope with the politics of
non-violence & bitter regrets. You laugh but the march of
history hates to lose.

Gleaming like the bellies of two fish a crab scuttles
viciously down an exposed spine. Egon Kisch lies
unremembered in a locked leaden coffin, sliding down
the silos of impotent reprimand. Stricken by the
pain of depression the 1940s end no sooner than
expected

I V

Birds change into tasteless clowns' mufti &
paint innately genocidal rhythms of random pattern.
Recidivists impose the basic wage which wars not
on poverty but allows what all fear: pervasive
postures of plutocratic indifference.
Murderous evasions have their day. Kindness & gentility
alike were sacrificed to the law of
lost opportunities. Barbarous looks & striped garter-snakes.

V

A black crazy mullah rips apart apathy like
rice-paper. Carter's attempts to invest reality with
a spectral majesty founder on
the grail of elusive belief. Goose-
bumps invite derision. Transparent sharks their teeth
gleaming like pylons circle each other silently in the
bathysphere

V I

Capitalism eats its own tale: the worm Ouroboros
speaking in tongues. We hear Americans bombing
another crazy dictator while
its institutions burn. With shame? With fear? No one
can say. The dialects of hate shake with joy
at the coming conflagration. Republican dreams
evaporate in an excess of self-congratulations,
somewhere in a desert, deep below
the sand, another worm
uncoils.

DIANE FAHEY
THE TWELVE DANCING PRINCESSES

In later life, none could recapture
  that long season of dancing nights –
   the enchanted risk of them:
     at twelve, the flight down steps;
       silk dresses rustling through groves
        of gold, diamond, and silver
       to the boat trip on moon-filmed water,
     the lake sighing and whispering its secrets
   as their perfect princes rowed them
  towards the underground castle
then danced the soles out of their shoes
  and plied them with wine
   and were impeccable
    as they rowed them home
     silent with ecstasy
       over the pear-shaped lake –
     princesses with dancing eyes
    returning to their locked room.
   Only the soldier who'd shadowed them,
  who'd stepped on the hem of the youngest
(her half-lit face half-turned)
  brought back mementos –
    three precious twigs and
     one of the goblets he'd emptied
      while partnering each princess
       invisibly, in his magic cloak.
      Then the exposé, the opulent evidence...
    The eldest was forced to marry him,
   the others became royal wives
  in far kingdoms where they had
balls and ballgowns to order.
  They glittered with riches
   and smiled convincingly
    but never again would they
     dance their slippers through.
      Strange jewellery they had made –
     gold leaves veined with diamonds
    and tiny silver twigs that they wore
   like open secrets. Often, too,
  they remembered the lantern
that sung across the lake

as if a star were caged in it.
In the cellar of the first castle
were heaped all the dancing shoes
full of centipedes and mice
and ropes of dust and mouldering
wine from a leaky cask
and old newspapers, sere
as parchment, and a book
with a rusty lock, containing
stories that sometimes ended,
"and the mouth of the last person
who told this story is still warm".

RON PRETTY
THE GLASS PIANO

I like him, she says, but he sets my teeth on edge
like running your fingernails against a chalkboard;
I don't mind him too much but he makes me nervous
minim after minim – a list of notes repeated
repeated, it sets my teeth on edge, like a kid
thumping a tennis ball against a wall, rain, rain
on an iron roof pattering, pattering, you don't mind
it but it gets to you, the same sound, the same pattern
of sound, hardly any variation, the minimum of change
it almost makes you nervous, sets your teeth on edge
like running your nails against a chalkboard,
like sex so boring it sets your teeth on edge
makes you wonder how you'll stand those first
gentle fingerings that go on and on, never changing much,
never reaching climax, slightly off like bacardi
and orange juice, or a politician kissing little boys,
elect me, I feel an election coming on, there's
a good boy, drink your orange juice while I kiss you,
the mother, her teeth on edge, fingernails on chalkboard
but flattered, the soft moth caress repeated,
repeated, the delicate minimalist fingertips
we like it but we're a bit on edge, fingertips soft
as a moth butting, butting against the glass, the teeth
set on edge, floating like moths against the window glass –
kiss me gentle as a moth or wanton boy . . .
I like him, but he makes me nervous (repeating)

This poem was first published in *Southerly* (Australia)

LORRAINE MARWOOD
JONAH, INSIDE

Basting in prayer
seaweed green and salty.

Jonah is praying underwater
all bubbles of words

drift through the Big fish's gills
like oars powering away.

Until the top of a wave
liberates the words, foam on a beach.

For three days, Jonah swims
within the fish, finding crevices

where the driftwood of a fish's years
catch near bone. Fine harp bones

and by the time Jonah is freed
he has composed many

songs of repentance, the resonance
is deep, even singing fathoms below

where starlight is a Creator's promise,
pinpoints so sharp that sea creatures

might think for one confused moment
that the Last day brought torture

instead of starlight shedding seed
through the darkest of subterranean caverns.

JILL JONES
THE DEAD TIDES

Water loves the moon, the dry captor.
Even behind the day it pulls
tides in the perfect gaze
of its dead face.
We forget in all our fret and forage
till we reach the edge, to be hunted by waves.

But even in our kitchens
dogs let us know something raw in us,
that feeds near where the bones live,
the rich coils of blood.
A map of how little distant we are
from rough grounds,
savage graves,
the watch fire on the mountain.

To the end we have reserved our tears,
pulled from us
by last moon at burial. They fight
in the flame,
in our anger at earth.

But from the dead these angers
pour away,
a last cry from the gape of the throat.
That day when lungs collapse
on the lake of the chest, the knot
of heart relaxes. There are no more tides
but the movement of stone
from one age to the next.

JOHN BENNETT
GREAT TOURIST DESTINATIONS
OF THE WORLD: NO. 197

A woman stands on her monumental shadow
scanning the precocious blue. I see that
the calcified units add a knife edge to the world.

Is this how far imagination has penetrated?
Fresh off the plane I was driven here
to jump into the Pacific and take its punctuations.

The Romantic cult of the South never reached
this latitude though there's an abundance of basic
commodities for one lifetime – past, presence and future.

From the bows of the Manly ferry, romantic hordes
point through the air and shoot the blue belly
of the harbour deserving the gift of tongues

and a gang of pensioners oblige by shouting
Cheese! in muddy Yorkshire accents.
Light somersaults across the water into eyes

sun licks the sandstone heads to honey
army barracks root the body back to bone.
Where the sky dips beneath a shaky blue line

flamboyant cornucopias of cloud well up
staining abruptly as shit daubs the horizon,
smog smothers this extended floating city.

A cruising seagull carries light like a spear
particles are caught in each barb of white feather,
each shapeless breath requires some weight of space.

DAVID McCOOEY
SIGNAL-TO-NOISE RATIO

The refrigerator keeps in time with cool darkness.
A video records, though the screen is blank.
Even the stereo cannot be silent.
Its lines are open and are noisy.
It listens to itself and hums.

This is locking up at night, *fin de siècle*.
Who knows what real silence is?
Outside, the city is in second gear.
I close the door and wonder
If it's true that things can express only themselves.

Only the clock, like time, seems silent;
Its LED flicking over with infinite indifference,
As if dealing out a pack of jokers.
My pen is rasping out a name I almost know.
And you? Can you hear me listening to myself?

ANTHONY LAWRENCE
THE CRYPTOGRAPHS OF THE HEAD

Under the blown circuitry of a winter sky,
          as three midges make the sign of the Trinity
                    then unstitch it, I consider

the useless analgesics of dependency.
          Somewhere near, Maria Callas
                    is darkening French windows

with a face her dying voice defines.
          Somewhere else, Finbar Furey
                    plays a memory of being

twelve years old, piping his way
          over the heart attack
                    of a punter at a Galway race meeting.

Chevron clouds disperse,
      leaving a washed blue mountain
            and its organ pipes of stone.

These distractions are brief.
      The loud ratchet of our anger is still
            drawing a frayed cable

of animated language through the house.
      I would offer you the red
            bonnets of canna lilies,

or a surfeit of drizzle
      from some expensive bottlemouth,
            but you crave what I do not have:

the essential skills of a well-adjusted man
      and more than this: honesty;
            the theoretical constancy of love.

Instead, I tell you that the marmoset,
      when cornered, smells
            of buttered popcorn;

that seagrass, in dusklight, appears
      as filaments of flathead blood.
            This is how I respond

to your desire for trust and change.
      Perhaps I am not capable of entering
            the slow contagion, of remorse

without poetry or some curious
      reference to the natural world.
            The empty shells of words, you say;

the cryptographs of the head.
      I respond with responsibility
            is an image I've been known to use.

ALISON CROGGON
FROM CAPRICES: MONSTERS OF REASON

All this was highly diverting for the five minutes it took to work out what was going on. For another minute, the observers amused themselves by ducking projectiles expelled from the anuses of the protagonists.

The angels of poetry rowed through the sky, tears rolling into their frail vessels. From here, they cried, we can see the shoulders of a young girl, shaking with laughter as she soaps herself in a porcelain bath. And here is an old man tending the relics of his youth, which glow in the shadows of his room with a peculiar and beautiful fatality. And there is still a stand of trees in a particular forest which has never witnessed the harsh doom of roads. But nobody listened.

They cried again: the world is roiled with poisonous smokes and the noise of explosions, and your streets are black with the sobs of aban-doned children, and the screams of lovers who hearts are split, and the wails of mothers and fathers whose babies are murdered before their eyes. And a great cold river runs through the heart of all the living, for those whom no one helped in their moment of need.

One would always like to imagine that shame silenced the battlefield. One is always imagining anything. But the truth is that nothing will stop them, for silence will remind them of their powerlessness. Consequently they have the generosity of piranhas, the astonishment of shoelaces and the compass of a pinhead.

It is only necessary to witness the obedience of those who carry their banners of freedom into mazes constructed with bureaucratic para-noia, to comprehend the despairs of our time. Where there are no walls, they import concrete and build them. Every door they find is padlocked shut. Intricate fields of barbed wire circle their cinematised foreheads.

Is life so cheap, that it must be this meanly spent? The proper response is, of course, compassion. But we are not always capable of propriety.

After all, nothing is more dangerous than a mediocre megalomania. At best, it will waste the time you do not have. At worst, it is the nightmare you never dared to imagine.

On Looking into the Australian Anthology

ROD MENGHAM ON JOHN TRANTER, JOHN FORBES AND GIG RYAN

JOHN TRANTER'S POEM 'On Looking Into the American Anthology' epitomizes the historical and geographical vertigo at the centre of Australian cultural identity. The title recalls Keats's 'On First Looking Into Chapman's Homer' but substitutes an anthological for a narrative text, replacing integration and coherence with the experience of disparate fragments. Tranter's project often includes poems on classical subjects which revolve around the incompleteness of textual evidence, providing conjectural translations within parentheses as well as frequent ellipses (see 'Papyrus'). The turn towards American culture requires a translation into Australian terms. For Keats, translation is necessitated by historical distance, a remoteness from Chapman almost as much as from Homer. For Tranter, the interval is spatial, a distance seemingly collapsed by international air travel but in fact upheld by cultural difference, the mutual untranslatability of Australian and American meanings being suggested by the different bearing given to the word "giant" at exactly corresponding points in each of the two sections of the poem: "'Giants Drank and Died Here'"; "the giant engines lift us". The dislocation of vocabulary results partly from the pressure to innovate in American culture, the desire to "Do it / First, and Do it Fast". Novelty soon leads to obsolescence, however; being first means being soonest out of date in a rapidity of turnover from which Australia seems far removed. The American "first" at the end of the first part is counterpointed by the Australian "last" at the end of the second: "The next stop – Australia – / is the end of the line". The poem's first setting is California, the second, mainly New Zealand. The focus of the California setting is a College professor stuffing fragments of America into his briefcase.

American culture is seen as obscure, as something that needs to be actively taught, made the subject of an official, if somewhat amateur, enquiry into the possibility of its being "Deep and Meaningful". This need for interpretation argues for the elusiveness of its object, its meanings apparently lost somewhere in transit, between centre and margins, between Hollywood and Auckland, between country and city. For the Australian observer in the nineteen eighties, America offers the most familiar version of otherness, but also the most narcissistic. For Tranter, the defining image is literally self-reflexive:

> Driving downtown he sees a pair of jugglers
> inch up the face of a glass cathedral full of
> marriages, mirrored in the noon glare, one on top,
>   and then his double.

Most of Tranter's poems about the transmission of cultural values, especially those with a classical theme, circle round this problem of self-reflexiveness and self-enclosure (see 'The Pool' and 'The Romans'). His Keatsian text is about looking, not "first" looking, partly because he needs to exploit the idea of being "first" in different ways, but also because his speaker looks at nothing unforeseeable; unlike Cortes, he is not struck dumb by the strangeness and immeasurableness of the scene. As a matter of fact, he reacts glibly, even though baffled by a lack of coherence; the poem characteristically strings together images and phrases whose relationship to one another is neither obvious nor inevitable. In the first part of the poem, the gaze of Cortes is replaced by the cleaners who see themselves reflected, married to their own images in an imaginary fulfilment of the narcissistic project. At the corresponding point in the second part, their counterpart is a figure who resembles a demented version of Keats himself, perhaps contemplating the destruction of his own Grecian urn. Tranter suggests how the interplay between permanence and transience, interaction and withdrawal, has become an intolerable tension, displacing Keats's anxious harmonies with a paralysing dissonance:

>   the shrill
> cacophony of jets rehearsing like a madman
>   staring at a vase.

Keats's urn makes an appearance at the end of John Forbes's poem 'Event Horizon' which also begins with a reference to Greek art:

> The Greeks invented the dust cover only to
> paint it / but we think of art as an alibi
> & see through it.

Art as a form of disguise we are meant to detect seems integral to Forbes's conception of Australian culture. Art figures in his work less in terms of status, value, subject matter or problems of technique than as an activity carried out in a certain space in relation to certain groups of people. And the space of Australian culture has the character of an alibi; it is always suspended between particular places, between different cultural habits and myths of origin; it pretends it is in one locale when really it is elsewhere; it is enunciated from somewhere near the locative case of the Latin word "alius" which means "other". Forbes's poetry is constantly posing the question of what authenticates Australian culture; and this gives rise to the image of the Australian author standing in other people's shoes. At crucial moments in the last fifty years, that country's literary history has been organized around spectacular frauds and forgeries, the constructing of alibis which have dramatically undermined the politics of ethnic and cultural identity. Except that they haven't, because the most authenticating currents in Australian culture have always been those which recognised the need for intersubjectivity, and for the constant recomposing of identity, generation by generation. Which is why the Pauline Hanson phenomenon is so absurd; it represents an Old World atavism that is less truly Australian than anything else. A project of metamorphosis, however, creates as much anxiety as exhilaration, produces a margin of insecurity in the transit from one state to another: the ghost of a syncopation haunting the rhythm of people's lives, something that "returns to bother them / like the ghost on a bad TV". The borrowed shoes of another tradition cease to look "sensible" in the Australian context: they either get "sprayed with beer / or [go] on a walking tour". Forbes's poems take the full measure of the beer-sodden stereotypes, only to itinerate away from them as energetically as possible. Although his subject matter is generally close to hand, just outside in the street, or inside on the screen, his poems move more restlessly and compulsively than those of any other urban ranger, evincing time and again the recognition that even in the heart of settlement, Australian culture has nowhere finally to settle, no space that its art could or should permanently occupy:

> no space
> remains for us to project ourselves into &
> we are on the outside, forever & here more

> beautiful than any illusion or act of love
> perfect because not breathing on a Greek vase.

That brilliantly equivocal last line, which both reproduces and recasts the ambiguity of the Keatsian original, attributes perfection to an art able to hold its breath for all time, while relegating that perfection in favour of the tarnishing breath of the vulgar. Forbes's own poetry is as breathful as its author was breathless, his and its respiration always audible. His extraordinary 'Love Poem', set against the Gulf War night-time bombing raids on Baghdad, demonstrates with exceptional clarity and succinctness the extent to which cultural identity is assured by being performed. It grafts the theatre of war onto the gestures of a frustrated lover, with a glibness that heightens the discrepancy between the two conditions. The smoothness with which the western television viewer is persuaded to identify with those in control of the military scenario both tempts and alienates the lover: "Our precision guided weapons / make the horizon flash & glow / but nothing I can do makes you / want me". His disempowerment is offset disturbingly by the unassertive, almost automatic, possessiveness of his relation to western aggression. The last line, "all this is being staged for me", is apparently ludicrous, but actually not so; the Gulf war merely accentuated the degree to which cultural identity both requires, and is vulnerable to, the conditions of public performance, some versions of which are more pernicious than others.

For Gig Ryan the performance of social identity is overdetermined by a whole range of different cultural conventions. In her poem 'Electra to Orestes', desire never finds the right object. The female speaker, for whom ancestry means too much, is rejected by one for whom the past means nothing. The language of the familiar and the familial, derived ultimately from Greek Tragedy, is overlaid by, and latticed with, an Elizabethan concern for value and face value. The conflict between true worth and meretricious allure is heightened by the application of a strict rhyme scheme (the poem is a sonnet), metrical discipline and period diction ("faithless sand he built an edifice on / and I colluded, mired in false trade"). The performance conventions of courtly address and paternalistic drama converge with the breezily masochistic narcissism of a more contemporary ideology: "My friend, before we met I was in pain... and so pretended for some paltry gain". Greek and

Elizabethan manners compete with the facetious idiom "no pain, no gain"; but the cultural density of these lines is oddly productive of an idiolect, a precarious individualism always on the verge of collapsing, yielding or retaining its margin of identity with the merest slip of the tongue: "not injured but inured." Ryan's idiolect is even more defiant and fragile in 'Achilleus to Odysseus', one of several poems in her new collection ghost-written by a literary composite:

> Vanished day,
> to strive for fame, to glitter in a marble pool
> but lose the task
> You sit among the virtuous weeding out life
> Personalities sulk
> the talking breakfast, the blacked-out calendar
> They whirl and fit

Extending and retracting, the verse moves between images of gregariousness and withdrawal. The great Homeric egoist in his tent addresses the archetypal itinerant in a language that rescinds all the usual distinctions between cosmopolitanism and isolation: "Drunken introverts graft home / the active and idle". The more extrovert Australian culture becomes, the more rapidly it discovers the self-centredness of Classical, English and American traditions, the extent to which its interlocutor is self-absorbed, obsessed with the need to "glitter in a marble pool". This narcissistic impermeability is where Tranter starts from and returns to, even while he cranes his neck to look over the gazer's shoulder. All three writers insist on cultural vagrancy, on a constant repositioning of historical and geographical markers. Even within the English dialect of the Australian vernacular, identity is both captured and released in the double exposure of failures to translate, valuably botched attempts to hold the alignments in place. Cultural development, so-called, cannot dispense with poetry in the business of alleging Australia.

IAIN BAMFORTH
HOPE, ART AND LABOUR

I

You have to court the namings, vagrant, go down Argent Street again
and pin the Declaration of the Citizen's Duties to the city hall,
let the gum-trees shed their pods into the Roaring Forties, the whale inflate itself
from Ayers Rock's red umbilicus, a special kind of contrivance
for allowing the id to float weightless and self-spectating, a reality-balloon.
Then fly the heft of it, the manila colour of a landmass
bursting with isotopes, that whole citric acid civilisation of juggernauts
advertising floaters and vast mineralogical undertakings.
Thus hitching the problem of who you are to where you're going, Chatwin-style,
though you're here to work, however many pioneers you galvanise.

II

Night lights up with stars, cold and crystalline, and the southern cross;
clarity in the world of things – it looks like a substitute for poetry
but isn't, is its occasion, though the seeping desert salt is killing arable land.
It means abandoned. It aims for the wafer words of inner drought:
infecund, sere, drained, leached, sucked dry, barren, issueless, jejune –
though you're out studying animal form, animals never seen before
like the visiting desert dragon, a creature from a Fellini film

that goes for weeks without water, and travels incognito till it lands up
inside a naked garden, landscape on its back. Also: sonny boy's first words,
Habakkuk it sounds like, a messenger between millennial zones.

III

Bushy pepper trees and bottlebrush flowers are probably covering up your tracks
but no worry, there's always an aggrieved exile in one of the watering holes
to remind you of your place, how clusters of tolerance work
out of poverty and hardship, and incredibly hard drinking aliases,
people on the point of abandoning their names in a bus shelter somewhere,
in a broken-down place they'd like to forget too near the centre
where they yearn and plant baroque cacti to the city life they're fleeing.
Australia of the open-air treatment. I'm watching people change
from one state to the next, but not their expressions, seeing how things erode
miles from sea or ship's furniture, here amidst the chemical flats.

IV

You're still bursting with love of it, and experience, still believing in hard work;
a decade gone, a memo addressed to the wife guiding you
across the city of the terror mines, scarlatina, cisterns with a sediment of lead;
the new police chief standing in the corner without his conversation hat
(not having needed one before), and beside him the god Hermes
sunstruck by the glare, an entire scrub-town, and the helix of your ears
straining for the sound of Bartley's Barrier Brass Band rounding the corner
Hope encouraging Art and Labour, under the influence of Peace.
What you get is Mario the circus barker drawing ribbons out of his mouth
as he walks across the baked turf of oysters shells and flint chips.

V

Years after still dreaming of the lemon tree and bougainvillea
in the neighbour's garden in Broken Hill, not dreaming so much as smelling
its singeing bush-breath, the same pungent scent of oil and alcohol
added to the flames of shaving by a Maltese, the town's sufferer of bad jokes,
his barber's E-number volatile above a dark green curtain of citrus leaves.
My field of vision takes in that, and the ways of bush baroque:
crankshafts in mining country, the ooze of time, salt mica, base materials.
Come and meet him then, ten years younger, a maverick setting out
with hope and high head, not yet a returnee, but already sure that looking back
the traveller sees as lengthening horizon what is, in fact, his aggregate.

THE REVIEW PAGES

Equerries of Doubt

MICHAEL HULSE ON TWO POETS ADDRESSING THE "AUSTRALIAN DILEMMA"

JOHN FORBES

Damaged Glamour

Brandl & Schlesinger
ISBN 1 876040 10 6

GIG RYAN

Pure and Applied

Paper Bark Press/Craftsman House
ISBN 0 9586482 6 3

WHEN JOHN FORBES, then in his early forties, published a stock-taking *New and Selected Poems* in 1992, it confirmed him as the third principal partner in that post-modern Australian triumvirate whose other slightly elder members were John Tranter and Robert Adamson. Efficiently backed by the Melbourne magazine *Scripsi* and by the *Penguin Book of Modern Australian Poetry* (edited by Tranter and Philip Mead, and published in this country by Bloodaxe), Forbes was formidable in his ability to dismantle the egotistical sublime, the attitudinizing of moral and political and aesthetic codes, and the dereliction (as he perceived it) of the lyric epiphany in poetry. The poem that closed that selection, titled (with a characteristic blend of irony and sincerity) 'Love Poem', found Forbes watching the Gulf War on TV: "I curl up with the war / in lieu of you [...] / I watch the west / do what the west does best // & know, obscurely, as I go to bed / all this is being staged for me".

In January 1998 John Forbes died of a heart attack, and *Damaged Glamour* is therefore presumably pretty much the last of his work we shall see, until the drafts that may still be in drawers or folders begin to attract the attentions of academic editors. His death was a substantial loss to Australian poetry: neither the line of Murray, Gray and Lehmann, nor the line of Tranter, Adamson and Gig Ryan, possesses anywhere else a writer so idiosyncratically able to bring an undercutting humour to bear on the fraught act we call poetry.

The fact is that Forbes was a moral (as well as a hedonistic) poet, a lyrical spirit, a writer of political, aesthetic and even spiritual conviction, and the satisfaction of reading him often derives directly from the strangely engaging spectacle of an astute intelligence dancing a sceptical jig around its own convictions.

So this posthumous collection find Forbes wondering, "if it's pitiful to waste your time, weeping / at the margins of your life, is it better // not to give a shit?" Did he think he had wasted his time weeping at the margins? He was an honest doubter, certainly. In 'Sydney Harbour Considered as a Matisse', he addresses the issue that was central to his life: reviewing a woman's number lipsticked on a crumpled Amex slip, a forex dealer fucking while he's on the phone, clouds and yachts and girls reduced to tears and blokes in sports cars fuming, he fetches up in the overwhelming question, "Can art be good enough to save all this, // plus the perfume of frangipani blooms / crushed on sandstone piers? Maybe just".

John Forbes hankered after the redemptive potential of art, I think, even as he found himself scarcely able to believe in that power, and it's this that makes his poetry so fully representative of the point the art has arrived at as the 20th century closes: already he is beginning to look like a seminal figure of the final quarter. But it's also his rhythmic appeal and the distinctive timbre of his personality that make him so readable, as well as an extraordinary epigrammatic flair that was clearly becoming more pronounced in his last work of the Nineties, as in 'Ode to Karl Marx':

Old father of the horrible bride whose
wedding cake has finally collapsed, you

spoke the truth that doesn't set us free –
it's like a lever made of words no one's

learnt to operate. So the machine it once
connected to just accelerates & each new

rap dance video's a perfect image of this,
bodies going faster and faster, still dancing

on the spot. [...]

In writers such as Forbes, Tranter and Gig Ryan we see in an acute form a dilemma that Australian culture inevitably saddles its poets with in these times: how to address the moment with the Roman confidence that writes odes and epistles, while at the same time remaining true to that international spirit of the age that knows doubt to be of the essence. The key poem in this dilemma is still David Malouf's 'Reading Horace outside Sydney, 1970', in which the sheer power of rhetoric marshals a magnificence in which a scraping goosequill two thousand years ago co-exists with a Cessna bi-plane crop-dusting lucerne. Among other things, Malouf's poem defines an important aspect of the Australian country-and-city experience, and suggests that Horace could indeed be the touchstone poet the continental nation has had most need of in recent years. Gig Ryan, I think, has come to a similar conclusion, albeit from that entirely different point of departure once described by Chris Wallace-Crabbe as an "essentially Melbourne line of expressionism", and with a preference for Petronius. Reviewing her third, mid-Eighties collection, *The Last Interior*, in *PN Review*, I was not entirely convinced by the pitch of her language; now I find myself wondering whether it might not be in her work, rather than in (say) Ashbery's or Manhire's, that post-modern poetry discovers its classical voice.

Ryan's work can seem daunting because it often resists paraphrase: behind the poems in *Pure and Applied* there are traceable narratives of European travel, of separation from a partner (bringing out a new directness of statement, such as "I want to go back to before I met you"), and so forth, but the direction in which the title points emphasizes that her art, like mathematics, can have a self-contained as well as a referential function. Even so, the strongest poems in this impressive book occur when available language and experience meet Ryan's sense that all language, perhaps all experience, exists in quotation marks, as it were. Poems begin "Unreal world ..." or "When I consider ..." and feature other familiar phrases ("change and decay") defamiliarized by contextual placing. Whole poems are given as speech inside inverted commas, on the lines of Lowell's "'To Speak of the Woe that is in Marriage'"; and Ryan's ear is superb. Her monologues have a fragmentary quality, as if spoken in a post-Poundian landscape littered with broken statues. These lines, from 'Petronius Arbiter in 1997', show to advantage her linguistic dislocations, her instinct for the satiric implications of voice, and the note of pessimism both cultural and personal that underlies, without disabling, most of her poems:

Do you like the jacket? I've just gone spare on
                            clothes
Materialism brooks and tastes after failure's screed
I'm post-delinquence. When money checked
I trashed it like a source, truth's zenith
I slate through the clubs, looking mint
where keen girls spot me like a crier on a plinth
a plastic card to deck, while spacey actors shift
But her cutting edge china, dinner an aubergine –
I undid the knot. I wish I was a saint
The writing comes all day in clots
I'm so drama. The air pinked passion
then devastation on a tab
All night I was conveyed, lobbied
to make a lesser mortal halt –
fabulous bachelor, equerry of doubts

Reverse Chronology

by Gig Ryan

**Australian Verse:
An Oxford Anthology**

edited by John Leonard
OUP
ISBN 0 195 50699 5

JOHN LEONARD'S INTRODUCTION states that "for the purposes of study" he has large selections from "five major 20th Century poets": Kenneth Slessor (1901-71), A. D. Hope (b.1905), Judith Wright (b.1915), Gwen Harwood (1920-95) and Les Murray (b.1938). Well-crafted though Harwood's work is, she does not consistently have the imagination or focus of either Christopher Brennan (1870-1932) or Francis Webb (1925-73) and is certainly a lesser poet than Peter Porter whose exclusion from this list is astonishing. For the purposes of study one should read every Australian anthology from the last 25 years to grasp who is missing from this anthology: Laurie Duggan, Pam Brown, Ken Bolton, Steve Kelen, Vicki Viidikas, Eric Beach, Jennifer Harrison, Ouyang Yu, Luke Davies, Adam Aitken, Tracy Ryan, Peter Minter, Morgan Yasbincek, John Mateer, Cassie Lewis to name a few. Without these poets, contemporary poetry looks a lot narrower than it is. His decision to reverse the chronological order is also disconcerting, and the anthology starts with the little-known Rebecca Edwards (b.1969). As well as Leonard's "major" five this anthology like most has its loyal squadron of poets counting time between developments, and though some poets can learn from bad poetry, presumably this book has a larger market.

There is not much emphasis on the more European or US-influenced poets. To these, John Tranter (b.1943) and John Forbes (1950–98) supplant Murray's nationalism. The scientific experiments beloved of Modernism are as a consequence thin on the ground here. The major 'Metaphysicals' – or Modernists – would be Brennan, Slessor, Wright sometimes, Webb, Tranter, Dransfield, Johnston, Forbes. Wright slips between both camps like a spy, as does Porter. Good poetry drags us out of the torpor of daily niceness by re-defining aesthetics, as in Webb's Shelleyan terza rima 'Morgan's Country' or Slessor's sonnets in 'Out of Time'

I saw Time flowing like the hundred yachts
That fly behind the daylight, foxed with air;
Or piercing, like the quince-bright, bitter slats
Of sun gone thrusting under Harbour's hair.

– or John Tranter's 1977 poem: "I'd like to throw an epilectic fit / at the Sydney Opera House and call it Rodent. / That's what separates me from the herd…" or John Forbes' 'Love Poems' – "Spent tracer flecks Baghdad's / bright video game sky / as I curl up with the war / in lieu of you…". Of poets born in the last 50 years, the late Michael Dransfield, Martin Johnson, Robert Harris, John Forbes and Vicki Viidikas now all seem more important, due partly to their early deaths, and one can hear unexpected echoes of Dransfield's cadences in some Philip Hodgins (1959-95). Other important modernists here are Robert Adamson, John Scott, and Alan Wearne.

Leonard's selection of Slessor and Wright are well-chosen. Wright is presented at her most varied, the once-radical Woman to Man (1949) poems, in which the creator-poet actually creates life, and 'At Cooloolah' which outlines her later political concerns:

but I'm a stranger, come of a conquering people.
I cannot share his calm who watch his lake,
being unloved by all my eyes delight in,
and made uneasy, for an old murder's sake.

as well as' To A Pastoral Family' and the dramatic monologue 'Eve to Her Daughers', but his selections of Hope and Harwood emphasise repetitiveness rather than variety. Hope's satirical bent is here kept in check, though his well-known 'Australia' (1939) is included:

And her five cities, like five teeming sores,
Each drains her: a vast parasite robber-state
Where second-hand Europeans pullulate
Timidly on the edge of alien shores…

Harwood's wit has generally been pushed aside in favour of sentiment, but 'In The Park' is here, "To the wind she says 'They have eaten me alive'". Murray is represented by one of his longest poems the 'Buladelah Taree Holiday Song Cycle', based on an Aboriginal song cycle, and the moving elegy 'The Last Hellos':

Grief ended when he died
the widower like soldiers who
won't live life their mates missed.

But Leonard has also chosed some of Murray's more bombastic works, which are not his best poems. Lesser-known poets are often misrepresented: Bruce Beaver, for example, would be better served without 'Eternity', Bruce Dawe is presented as a bland chronicler rather than a biting satirist, Tony Linterman's embarrassing imitation of Christopher Smart has been included but not Martin Johnston's 'In Memoriam' ("where the blood pours out the dead come to the feast") or Forbes' 'On the Beach: a Bicentennial Poem', Mark O'Connor's nature poems but not Vicki Viidikas's urban grunge. The selection of Jennifer Maiden (b.1949) makes her more conventional than she has been and John Kinsella's two small poems are unrepresentative. Leonard's bias is towards the accessible, the "heartfelt", and so there are many flaccid and sincere poems that do not engage attention.

Exciting re-discoveries are the 19th Century poems of rage and protest, such as Eliza Hamilton Dunlop's 'The Aboriginal Mother', published during the controversy of the Myall Creek Massacre (1838) – controversial because some white men responsible for the massacre of aborigines were hanged – or the pseudonymous Hugo's 'The Gin' which overturns the notion of "terra nullius" long before 1992's High Court Judgement.

Like Porter's *Modern Australian Verse* (1996) Leonard has also excluded translations of Aboriginal songs and poem but he has done a great service in bringing fresh poems to light from Marie F. J. Pitt (1869-1948), Dorothea Mackellar (1885-

1968), Mary Fullerton (1868-1956), Mary Gilmore (1865-1962) and Zora Cross (1890-1964). Harry Kendall (1839-82) and John Shaw Neilson (1872-1942) also look better here than in other anthologies, as do R. D. FitzGerald, James McAuley, Elizabeth Riddell and Dorothy Hewett.

Generally, older poets fare better than the younger in Leonard's selections, and for a more varied view this anthology should be read alongside other anthologies: Tranter-Mead's *Modern Australian Poetry* (1991), Murray's *Australian Verse* (revised, 1991), Lever's *Australian Women's Verse* (1995) and Porter's *Modern Australian Verse* (1996).

Borders & Crossings

by Katherine Gallagher

FAY ZWICKY

The Gatekeeper's Wife

Brandl & Schlesinger, (no price given)

ISBN 1 876040 04 1

ADAM AITKEN

Crossing Lake Toba

Folio (Salt) Pamphlet Series, £2.50 & postage
ISBN 1 901994 93 7

ALISON CROGGON

The Blue Gate

Black Pepper Press, (no price given)
ISBN 1 876044 18 7

DIANE FAHEY

Listening to a Far Sea

Hale & Iremonger, (no price given)
ISBN 0 86806642 7

S.K. KELEN

Postcards from the Universe,

Folio (Salt) Pamphlet Series, (£2.50 & postage)
ISBN 1 901994 56 2

THE 1980s AND 1990s represent a broadening out of the Australian poetry scene with room for a wider range of voices. Not before time, but it has happened, helped along by the publication of redoubtable anthologies such as *The Penguin Book of Australian Women Poets* (1986), and *Inside Black Australia* (1988). During the nineties, OUP (Australia) has been particularly active in bringing out splendid anthologies edited by Les Murray, Peter Porter, Jennifer Strauss and Susan Lever respectively. In 1994, there was Bloodaxe's publication of John Tranter and Philip Mead's (1991) *Penguin Book of Australian Verse*. And there have been Special Issues such as this British one, alongside greater opportunities for individual Australian poets to have their work published here or at least distributed over here.

"Old poets never die, they just blaze away", Judith Wright is quoted as saying, whilst noting on another occasion that in writing poetry, she hadn't been able to reach as many as she would have if she'd been writing prose. And great environmentalist that she is, that wasn't enough. Nevertheless, her spirit is trailblazing for the collections under review here. This is particularly true of those of Zwicky, Fahey and Croggon, who represent three generations after Wright's, and in their way, epitomise the bringing in of women's poetry from the margins.

The Gatekeeper's Wife is Zwicky's first collection since her *Poems: 1970-1992*. What is remarkable about Zwicky is her range which extends from lyrics to satires to parodies. She is much concerned with love, alienation, relationships, memory and death, casting a wide eye over it all:

Keeping the pen on the move
keeps you somewhere near.
It writes against our oblivion.

('Orpheus')

In her poetry, Zwicky, the ex-concert pianist, technically adroit, dramatic and profoundly serious, is always there alongside the joker, the edgy ironist making wry asides against the world, patriarchy and herself. Her formal poems sit easily beside her mostly short-lined, tightly-wrought free verse. Her cadences are a delight.

Zwicky has used displacement to examine her Jewishness, reflected back in family portraits as well as moving elegies for public figures such as Primo Levi and Allen Ginsberg, "hymning his dead, his wrecked / mescalin fired-up generation" ('Groundswell for Ginsberg').

In this latest book, Zwicky displays a new vulnerability, and, particularly in her relationship-poems, a new awareness of death and ageing. Of a fairly recent portrait done of her by the artist Louis Kahan, she notes, "Too much dying, too much growing up in that face..." ('Portrait'). This more reflective side of her is balanced by witty pieces such as 'A Laureate Comes to Lunch' and 'Letter from Claudia in the Midi' where she satirises the situation in a tone reminiscent of Gwen Harwood's excursions with Professor Krote. Irony is her forte, and the barbs, even half-kindly ones, are always ready. Again, this acerbic side of her work must be seen against her more poignant pieces – for example, the love poems for her late husband, with their lyrical immediacy and openness:

Newly married! Newly married!
sang the motor bike to dust
puffs rising from our dash.
We were, and how I wished to be.

('Perdjodohan')

A frequent prizewinner for her poems, Fay Zwicky has just shared with John Kinsella the 1999 Western Australia Premier's Award for Poetry for *The Gatekeeper's Wife*. Zwicky's multi-faceted, assured poetry deserves to be much more widely known.

Diane Fahey, who published her first collection in 1986, is an adventurous poet, always investigating new fields, surfaces, including the territories of myth, domesticating them with ruthless intelligence, passion, and a clear eye, in tones that range from the tragic to the irreverent to the comic. In an earlier book, *Metamorphoses* (1988), she presented feminist reworkings of classical myth, particularly from the point of view of man–woman relationships. In this, her sixth book, she sails into wider seas, looking especially at the myth of the hero, alongside other general human failings. The patriarchy – war, business, family, success and failure – is her subject, and Fahey showers us with recognitions in a sardonic tone that is sometimes sad, sometimes savagely comic. 'The Graeae', quoted in full, gives the flavour:

Yet another set
of women in triplicate...
They share an eye and a tooth between them –
a capacity the well-run modern state
might wish for many of us.

And what are these women doing?
They are creating
a history of the world.

The facts take them a long time to digest,
and it is a strain writing by a single candle,
with a single eye,

but they have three minds,
each of them razor-sharp
well-used to remembering, anticipating,
        the smallest light in any darkness.

The success of the poems in this collection derives from Fahey's ability to imagine parallels and situations, both classical and contemporary, to fit various myths, and to give them a dramatic twist. There is great skill and assurance in this, as Fahey's resonant voice – challenging, wry, breakaway, lays open paradoxes, not least the no-win madness of violence, war and random killing:

The host's three sons slain
for serving the wrong
portion of the beast...

What's for dessert,
and who will serve it?

('Heracles' Lunch')

Occasionally, Fahey's lively touch deserts her. In 'Prometheus', the god's despairing question about what has been proved by his ritual fire-eating and various feats, is followed by this recognition: "The answer comes back:/That I am a god,/unkillable". This is rather matter-of-fact. No doubt, Fahey was bored by him.

My favourites among her poems are her more personal works such as those from her 1995 collection, *The Body in Time*. Diane Fahey is a wide-ranging accomplished poet, highly deserving of her growing international reputation.

Alison Croggon, (b. 1962), novelist, playwright, as well as poet, is a passionate and engaging voice. *The Blue Gate* is her second collection. Croggon's is an intensely personal poetry – sensitive, elemental, bordering on the mystical, and cloaking a terse vulnerability. Her poetry is mostly in short-lined or long-lined free verse but she also has a group of sonnets that show an easy mastery of this form. Croggon is also a playwright and sometimes her meditations have the packed questing of poetic monologue: "Let me say without self-pity, that I love a man / who loves me more than sanity can bear" ('Sonnets I').

Alison Croggon

Her poems, even when she is using very simple imagery, can be wonderfully charged and erotic:

> Light breathes out into this room
> that I have made my own. I think of you
> and how only yesterday you kissed the skin
> inside my wrist, the blue private skin
> where my blood runs closest to the air.
>
> ('Prayer')

Her love poems, including those for her children, are tender and especially moving, with a fiery expansiveness reminiscent of Nina Cassian. Occasionally, the effect can be overwrought, as in ('Bearing') or too slight as in ('Limbo'). But who couldn't be excited by her long lines in the Whitmanesque 'The Elwood Organic Fruit and Vegetable Shop' to which she goes walking "with (her) mind as smooth as a marrow / winking at the unruffled sky throwing its light down for free".

John Kinsella and Tracy Ryan's Folio (Salt) Editions Pamphlet Series along with their magazine *Salt*, are providing a fine service in bringing to notice work by Australian and other poets unknown in the U.K., except possibly through the Internet. Pamphlets are always extremely useful for poets in between books, as is the case here with Adam Aitken and S.K. Kelen.

Aitken's *Crossing Lake Toba* presents poems seamed with telling detail where the new, meaning Western-European/Asia Inc., meets the Third World South-East Asian lifestyle.

The poems, headed by epigraphs about Headhunting, are closely packed around a theme of change versus exploitation, (the question of Who's headhunting who?) and work by a tightly controlled use of irony and juxtapositions. Aitken's voice is understated, but eloquent in his criticism of the exploitation of these peoples and their livelihoods. In 'Graves', the country being visited appears familiar: "It could be Tropical Norway (satellite TV version) /....Hothead locals pose in our image of elsewhere. /... /No fences, no visible boundaries. Their machinery is a buffalo". The tone is relentless, poignant, reminding that we're all global now...

S. K. Kelen's *Postcards from the Universe* also focuses, as the title suggests, on scenes from a journey. He ranges widely, from singing the rainforest in Australia, 'The Mountain Walk', where "The echidnas curl up disguised as baby trees" to Wales, and the U.S.

Keenly-observed, these poems celebrate the gusto of everyday life, note various quirks and excesses: I especially liked his snapshot of New York, with its "...music of cars and people / Who go about their business, / Eat everything, drive fast / Take their high rise hounds / To the dog run in the park". As he says, not without irony, "It's a high-minded city / That can give to animals".

Folio (Salt) pamphlets are available from John Kinsella, Churchill College, Cambridge CB3 0DS.

Dumb Ministry

by David Wheatley

ROBERT GRAY

Lineations

Arc, £8.95

ISBN 1 900072 09 2

ROBERT CRAWFORD ONCE joked that getting Australian poetry into the UK was like trying to get a Qantas flight into Auchtermuchty. Things have improved since then, to the point where the Australian poets in print in the British isles today include A. D. Hope, Judith Wright, Dorothy Hewett, Les Murray's *Fivefathers*, Murray himself, David Malouf, John Kinsella, John Tranter, Dimitris Tsaloumas, Kevin Hart, and while OUP stocks last, Peter Porter, Chris Wallace-Crabbe and Gwen Harwood. Nevertheless, the list of Australians you won't find in Auchtermuchty or anywhere else over here is depressingly long: Bruce Dawe, Bruce Beaver, Robert Adamson, Adam Aitken, Philip Hodgins, Philip Salom, Jemal Sharah and Peter Rose, to name but a few. Robert Gray (b. 1945) has three poems in Tranter and Mead's *Penguin Book of Modern Australian* Poetry, but for most of us *Lineations* will be a first extended introduction to this melancholy imagist of New South Wales.

To judge from the teeming Malley-Ashbery hybrids in the second half of the Penguin Book, Gray is in many ways an atypical Australian poet. In Britain and Ireland postmodernist poetry still hangs around the fringes, only penetrating the broadsheets when a large publisher takes a risk with a book like *Conductors of Chaos*. Since John Tranter's hectic efforts on its behalf in the sixties and seventies, Australian postmodernism is, if not *the* at least *a* cultural norm. This in turn has had an effect on the non-postmodernists, inspiring a worried defensiveness where most British and Irish poets would be simply oblivious: it's hard to imagine Seamus Heaney or Tony Harrison spending as much time as Les Murray does crusading against elitist modernism. Gray lacks Murray's appetite for versified polemic, but belongs in the same anti-modernist camp along with Jamie Grant, Kevin

Hart and Philip Hodgins. Where John Kinsella might take off on a syzygy, Gray keeps to the straight and narrow, constantly touching base with his verities and "going straight for the pay-dirt of emotion", as he praises Hodgins for doing.

Gray is strong on landscape, picking out detail after detail like "flaws / in the weathered canvas of the plains": the "thistle-tops" of car headlights coloured "refrigerator blue", sparrows tipping "briefly as a pepper pot", the "sad industry / of crickets / [...] in recession / once again". Despite those crickets, these are poems in which the eye rules supreme: "My life, I imagined, must be a hymn / to the optic nerve". Imagism is a basically intransitive aesthetic, well suited to the oriental terseness of '10 poems' and 'Travelling', but more difficult to sustain over longer stretches. It's no surprise then to find him turning to an oriental subject and style when he wants to write a narrative, in 'The Life of a Chinese Poet'.

Another side of Gray that staves off imagist monotony is his taste for aphorism. In 'Illusions' and 'Epigrams' he comes out with some very unpostmodernist certainties and *touchés*, as when he trades motes and beams with smug experimentalists:

> *Épater les bourgeois?* Certainly,
> but there is another complacency one mustn't
> overlook. *Épater les avant-gardistes.*

At times he gives us a Zen version of early Mahon, wistfully contemplating a disused petrol pump or straining to hear the "dumb ministry" of "natural things" (cf. Mahon's 'The Mute Phenomena'). When he progresses to full-blown philosophy though, as in 'A Testimony', he reads like Hardy without the cosmic *Schadenfreude*: "Existence must come of itself, and it goes on and on without a reason, just because it is. / [...] It has arrived where it might understand. Perhaps it cannot bear this". Perhaps not, but few readers will find the discovery as exciting as his observations of birds in flight or ripples on the Hawkesbury river. A sweeping proposition about the vanity of human wishes is not the same thing as a sweeping line of poetry.

The best of Gray is in poems such as 'Malthusian Island', where he gets his allegory just right, 'The Life of a Chinese Poet', 'In one ear...', 'A Pine Forest', 'The White Roads' and 'On A Forest Trail'. He is at his strongest in epiphanies of detail and precision clung on to in the face of a comfortless world, and at his weakest when he gives in to prolixity and inflated commonplaces to fill out the space between them. Maybe his *New Selected Poems* (1998) would have made a better British début. If Arc keep delivering with their International Poets Series, Gray should have a trick or two left for the folks in Auchtermuchty.

Travels in the Inback

by Ian McMillan

PHILIP SALOM

New and Selected Poems

Fremantle Arts Centre Press
ISBN 1863682 18 X

TOM SHAPCOTT

The Sun's Waste is Our Energy

Folio/Salt Press, £2.50 + 50p p&p

I HAD THIS legendary great uncle who disappeared. He walked into the vastness of Australia and just disappeared, sometime early this century. I feel a bit like him as I wander about in the vastness of Philip Salom's poetry, because I always like to imagine that my Great Uncle wasn't actually lost, but that he just enjoyed the view and didn't want to leave, and that's exactly how I feel about this book.

Philip Salom wasn't known to me at all before I got this book: he was born in 1950 and he's been writing for years and years, publishing books since 1980. He's lived and worked all over the place, although he currently lives in Melbourne, but reading the book you certainly get a sense of a citizen of the world.

Salom's poems are a bit like those 'Eat All You Can' restaurants so beloved of Homer Simpson and me; they're full to bursting with long lines, fat stanzas, huge ideas, as in 'The Man Who Mistook His Wife For A Hat', which is just one big stanza, and which opens with "The Mind is the biggest city of all / and every suburb: hope, ambition, greed, / and a dozen others, the grim / or the rich localities – are

hung each night on memory". Those are neatly emblematic Salom lines, encompassing the aforementioned big ideas, but also a listy (the poetic equivalent of lusty) need to Get Everything In, to expand on the City of the Mind idea, to stretch it as though is was a rubber band. This wordyness isn't a bad thing, though, and I'm not saying that a stripped-down Salom would be a good idea; his eagerness to tell the story or to paint the scene carries you along with it as though you're a canoe and he's the whitewater.

The poems are about travel ("There are heads poking out of boxes, / feather stains and cat stalls, the high reek / of durians thickening under roof-iron" from 'Wet Markets Singapore') sex ("I've kissed your neck and you've arched / like a vault. We've echoed like hillsides / on a summer night" from 'Music and Stone') and, for want of a better word, Nature ("I see one / magnificent fish, primal / gold in waters dark as oil / supple scales deepening into the green" from 'The Fish'). I even found someone who could have been my great uncle, sadly dead in a grain store: "at the granary, / staring at a man drowned in the grain, / dark nostrils filled with wheat / his throat blocked from swallowing, begging for air"(Jezba).

After the stacked plate of Salom, Tom Shapcott's pamphlet is like one of those little appetisers you get in posh places. Shapcott is a bit Salomish in that he likes long lines and big statements: "Her dream is to stand in the midst of everything / with a silver comb in her hair and a bauhinia / resting like a butterfly on her shoulder", but within the skinny volume format he doesn't really have room to stretch. The most successful poems are the ones like 'The Ghost Rock Pool', (a sestina!) which take images, in this case of office workers thinking of talking a dip in water ("We lived in the imagination of that place, that country / rockpool surrounded by shade trees, with ice-deepwater / below the surface where bottlebrush pollen would settle / and insects would hover"). It sounds like the kind of place my Great Uncle would have liked...

Shambling Contingencies

by Brian Henry

PETER ROSE

Donatello in Wangaratta

Hale & Iremonger, $A16.95

ISBN 0 868 06654 0

GIG RYAN

Research

Folio (Salt), £2.50

CORAL HULL

Broken Land: 5 days in Bre

Five Islands Press, $A12.95

ISBN 0 864 18450 6

CORAL HULL

How Do Detectives Make Love?

Penguin, $A19.95

ISBN 0 140 58768 3

PAM BROWN

My Lightweight Intentions

Folio (Salt), £2.50

ISBN 1 901 99423 6

ALTHOUGH READERS TOO often equate poetic elegance and sophistication with formal competence, Peter Rose repeatedly proves the possibility of elegance within free verse. His technique lends his poems the kind of suppleness – a posture of ease – that we find in poets like John Ashbery or Frank O'Hara. Although Rose has learned much from the Americans, his cultural references, satiric penchant, and European and Australian concerns most recall the expatriate Peter Porter. But Rose – born, reared, and residing in the state of Victoria – must content himself with imaginary or temporary jaunts abroad while focusing on the life in front of him. The result is a distinctively Australian poetry that continually pines for elsewhere.

Operating by the principle "always the simplest phenomena / giving most pleasure", Rose focuses on the transitory in an attempt to notice what we usually overlook. His third collection, *Donatello in Wangaratta*, opens with a typically marginal gesture – "Let's not watch the main event, / let's watch the people" – and then proceeds through an intimate yet public world of love and loss that celebrates the "fortitude of isolates". Rose's powers of observation, evident throughout the book, emerge most suggestively when, in the manner of Cavafy, he slyly eyes young men: "a handsome / young man dawdling beneath / his flat, smoking a last cigarette, / as if remembering someone / sacrificed in a previous city". Frequently for this voyeuristic poet, "night / brings no rigors of embrace, / no twisting blanditude".

The tensions that Rose establishes – between evasion and confrontation, movement and stasis, restlessness and contentment – also emanate from the homosexual desires driving some of the poems. The book's title poem is an initiation into carnal knowledge facilitated by a photograph of Donatello's David:

> you finger my new red Caxton encyclopaedia,
> perplexed at such a gift (for I am six),
> turn the page, a robe on enlightenment,
> reveal David gleaming, audacious,
> uniting us in his slim mimicry.

At the end of the poem, this precocious sexual awakening acquires a distinct religious element, thereby linking sex and belief: "And suddenly the room is alight, / fired with its own brazen iconography, / silencing and separating as it unites ... / reshaped in its own tense and furtive imagery".

Donatello in Wangaratta contains many "beautifully private" love poems in which the beloved is present as a reference more often than as a person. This obliqueness foregrounds the role of perception and the illusion of shared knowledge generated by the poet, "amorously stung" yet "itinerant as light". With its indeterminate polyphony, 'Self-Portrait in Non Sequiturs' embodies the disembodied talk of the office (Rose works in book publishing) but manages to end with an articulation of desire:

> Joseph has so far to go, they shake their heads in
> Marketing.

She places it beautifully, don't you think?

I'll be in the library if you need me.

...

So much for silent numbers.

The hands of a saint, if you know what I mean.

I can get it for you wholesale.

You'll hurt yourself doing it that way.

Too many quotes, too many footnotes altogether.

My last glimpse of him was in a mirror. Imagine.

The various tones, the pronouns with their uncertain antecedents, the commingling of public speech and private communication, the implications and understatements and blunt offers characterize Rose's poetry in general, but make this aptly titled self-portrait one of the book's most inventive and notable poems.

Although Rose engages the topics of love and lust in many of these poems, he is also concerned with how "we are all cancelled in the end". His elegies for the poets James Merrill and Philip Hodgins convey the pain of loss without losing sight of the poet's responsibility to language. In a poem about a failed relationship (not his own), Rose writes about "the rictus of sadness / that makes you look away". His own emotional situations, "hopeless and erotic at the same time", counterbalance the civilised desires that generally drive the book, "yearning for interstices of night, / ... beautifully registered, beautifully going on".

In contrast to Rose's decorous style, Gig Ryan's poems in the pamphlet *Research* pursue a twisted romanticism. They rely on the self and the self's weathers for their sustenance, but when "My heart my brain are all locked up", the poems ultimately discard the more emotive elements of lyric poetry. "Full of icy self-regard", Ryan's persona leads anything but an "undiagnosed life". This clinical language seems appropriate for a poet whose persona emerges as cynical and stringent, especially when she skewers whatever fails to conform to her version of morality. Ryan might be politically progressive, but the severe tone in her poems can undermine her social conscience, however sincere. Some of her earlier poems, particularly those from *The Last Interior* (1986), don a persistent sneer at those less self-aware than the poet's persona, and are therefore disturbing in their determination to hold onto some kind of superiority. Less problematic than some of her earlier poems, *Research* is nonetheless complicated by the poet's attempt to maintain the upper moral hand.

Because of Ryan's solemnity, the occasional humorous moment acquires a cathartic energy disproportionate to its frequency: "I enjoy the government art, visionary and affirming"; "Anxiety thrives on a high income"; "gangs of rubbish guard the useful block". But these poems are intent on incisive political and social commentary: "Our Prime Minister shuffles and prevaricates / Let's lose the black armband glitch of history / and praise our forebears, clanking through shiny trees / and taming soil. Here we plant democracy". Acutely aware of the subtleties of language, Ryan often loads her adjectives with irony or judgment: "the green pool's vacuous beauty", "gentle machines water the streets", "on television a leader's doctored face", "his slippery violin amongst the brawling TV sets", "another sparkling execution". Distinctive and frequently stunning, such uses of language refuse to affirm; rather, they inform readers about what the poet stands against: she is anti-urbanization, -technology, -imperialism, -media, -hypocrisy, -ignorance, and -suburbia. For all her stylistic innovation, Ryan is, above all, a didactic poet, more determined to educate (and sometimes chastise or implicate) her readers than to delight them.

With the exception of two sonnets (one Petrarchan, one of Ryan's invention), the poems in *Research* are written in a disjunctive free verse. Through their halting progression and idiosyncratic punctuation and capitalization, they reveal an abiding distrust for eloquence and polish without rejecting lyricism. Ryan's style consciously subverts her own music while establishing it:

> I couldn't get the hook or when it was
> Penultimately I had to blank
> Another day to quail, a vice to con for him
> Freedom was a drink
> as if it killed me
> ('Research')

Ryan's innovative stylistic strategies have remained consistent and singular since her first book. What she loses in variety and range, she gains in distinction. Perhaps because the form generally insists on closure, her sonnets in *Research* – 'When I consider' and 'Not ecstasy, but anxiety' – veer from her usual rejection of epiphany and, in turn, benefit from Ryan's sharp lyricism and the linguistic, aural, emotional, and logical possibilities of the sonnet. In the sonnets, she seems less intent on thwarting lyricism than on harnessing its potential, evident in the final sestet of 'When I consider':

> I pause at the silky prolonged sunset
> that death or god should taper off
> > and shrink
> as all the city's woe and all the
> > skies
> say not to remember but to forget
> and chafing through the cars I
> > fall to think
> how sorrows lift and pleasures
> > cauterize

Although her other poems contain striking imagery, metaphor, and phrasing, they seldom cohere or convince through their fragmentariness. In their rejection of resolution and cohesion, many of Ryan's poems seem most powerful in their parts, carrying a lot of weight but too little pleasure.

As politically and socially aware as Ryan, Coral Hull, in *Broken Land: 5 days in Bre*, emerges as more journalistic. Where Ryan's poetry is obviously written in the language of poetry, Hull's frequently resembles prose, and lacks the linguistic friction that contributes to Ryan's work. Hull's prosaic style most likely reflects the book's project – to chronicle a town "on its last legs" – more than her own limitations, since she clearly privileges the message over the medium throughout the book. The poet here adopts the role of witness, and at one point even says "I don't need a camera. / I take photos with my heart", with little or no irony.

A book of observation and feeling, *Broken Land*, in its combination of testimony and personal experience, emulates Muriel Rukeyser's *U.S. 1* or, more recently, John Kinsella's anti-pastoral poetry. Hull's capacity for recording others' speech and her talent for description comprise the book's primary strengths. By recording all that she sees, hears, smells, and feels, Hull succeeds in capturing the moribund yet rough spirit of the place and its inhabitants, set on killing the land and most of the animals on it. In the first half of the book, she explores her difference from the locals, and then proceeds to itemize and bemoan the destruction of the fauna and flora in poems such as 'The Goat Abattoir', 'The Dark Dead Blood of the Kangaroo', 'A Dead Fox on the Grid Sign', and 'Wildflowers at Bre'. She also exposes anti-aboriginal racism in Bre without editorializing: "The whole town watching the house burn down. / The fire brigade in Bathurst Street took their time. / It must be a black fella's house".

Despite her admirable aims, Hull's writing can disappoint. After being harassed by the workers in a kangaroo boning factory, the poet predictably compares herself with the butchered animals:

> I felt like a kangaroo when they
> > whistled & called out
> ... I was unaffected by them.
> Undecapitated, non-disemboweled.
> They hadn't ripped my heart out
> or broken my ribs & spine.
> They hadn't cut me open or stuck
> > their hands inside.
> Or crushed my spirit into the ground
> > as bone or glass.
> Or strung me up or sold me to the petfood industry.
> Or slapped me down, or taken my young.

In her efforts to be all-encompassing here, she neglects the idea with the most potential for exploration – the connection between rape and slaughter – thereby rendering the moment nearly superfluous: she is most likely preaching to the converted. Similarly, readers do not need to be told "The stink of flesh stayed with me for days" or "There is evil" in the factory. Hull is more effective when more subtle. When not weakened by obvious messages, *Broken Land* is sometimes diminished by the prevalence of redundant or verbose writing:

> The kind of dog that cannot be trusted anymore.
> That could bite the hand that feeds him.
> Because in the past
> the hand that fed him
> has also beaten him up.
> ... I also think his owner should not beat him up &

> Most of Brown's poems rev at high speed yet take their time in reaching their destinations. For Brown, "writing a poem" becomes a "shambling contingency", an act fraught with uncertainty.

he should go to a dog shrink.

Hull also can be trite and unimaginative, as when she describes the effect of a goat's scream on her: "I have never heard it before & I never want to hear it again. / But for now I must hear it forever".

Fortunately, in her other recent collection, *How Do Detectives Make Love?*, Hull succeeds in establishing and sustaining a unique style. The most visible technique – punctuation mainly by slashes – is complemented by the use of ampersands and lack of capitalization, which give these poems flexibility: throughout the book, Hull vacillates between narrative and lyric modes without straining her resources. Many poems progress non-fluidly while others generate explicit narratives. Although these poems infrequently benefit from the torque and tension made possible by line breaks, the pervasiveness of honed, memorable lines and phrases distinguishes the book.

As in *Broken Land*, Hull depicts a brutal Australia in *How Do Detectives Make Love?*, and shows that humans (especially men with their "ruined sexualities & undone emotions") can be the least humane of animals. These poems, particularly the end of 'Twin Rivers – Thunder, Lightning & Wind', also demonstrate Hull's descriptive strengths, all the more convincing for the absence of tendentious commentary:

everything loosens & shakes at the sky blown

forwards/

& the storm is thrown down over the land leavings

its

silence behind/ & the next day a magpie appears in the blueness to sing out in the silence & a kangaroo thumps the dust with her heavy red tail

"In search of clearer weather", Hull nevertheless is drawn to rumination, an act often muddled by the limitations of memory and of reason. The poems in *How Do Detectives Make Love?* are more unsettling than those in *Broken Land* because of the psychological darkness coloring many of them. This attention to the workings of the mind produces complex and satisfying poems – 'Affinity', 'The Statue', 'An Hour After Suicide', 'Royal Park Stalker Sequence'. Hull's persona, though identifiable with the poet, continually changes, recalling the difficulties of adolescence in one poem and stalking a stalker in the next. This variety holds self-indulgence at bay while insisting on the validity of autobiography as a subject for poetry.

The title of Pam Brown's *My Lightweight Intentions* is simultaneously self-effacing, descriptive, and ironic. With its short lines and obsessions with the quotidian, her poetry might appear lightweight (and at 22 pages this pamphlet is), but her approach ultimately justifies its subjects. Because Brown's poems often extend to three or four pages, a pamphlet of this size seems insufficient ground on which to come to terms with her work.

Most of Brown's poems rev at high speed yet take their time in reaching their destinations. For Brown, "writing a poem" becomes a "shambling contingency", an act fraught with uncertainty. Because she highlights the means of the journey (the process of composition), this leisurely manic pace usually requires several pages to satisfy. Therefore, a short poem like "A howling in favour of failures...", despite some strong lines, relies too much on its punch-line ending, a tactic that gives more pleasure when the poet has established a larger space in which to roam.

Although Brown sometimes resembles a late-generation New York School poet ("customised / fragments organizing a stanza / in public!", "disappointed by / my century's / pragmatics, / I declare / the age of riesling") or a Sydney poet ("even the rubbish / appears artificial", "o no it's / an index of anecdote"), she is always a humorous, iconoclastic, and observant one: "taking so long / to write the book – / only to be / remaindered", "the glory / white fringes / of the green & red / umbrellas / sussurate". Despite her affinities, Brown has developed her own blend of disillusionment, tenderness, social criticism, and self-criticism, as in 'Miracles', one of the most remarkable of the seven poems in the pamphlet:

Condemned to fidelity,
    they trail along
        blindly – into ennui,
and into boringness,
assembling
    dull catastrophes
in the shadowiest recess
    where gems
    could
        glow...

Because of her refusal to "trail along blindly", Brown's poems do glow. They just need a wider expanse in which to shine.

THE CLASSIC POEM

2. SELECTED BY FRANK KERMODE

I WOULD HAVE preferred 'An Epistle: Edward Sackville to Venetia Digby', a fine example of pastiche 17th century epistle form, a wonderfully controlled and great poem, but that was precluded by its length. 'Imperial Adam' shows the bitter exuberance that Hope sometimes generates.

A. D. HOPE
IMPERIAL ADAM

Imperial Adam, naked in the dew,
Felt his brown flanks and found the rib was gone.
Puzzled he turned and saw where, two and two,
The mighty spoor of Jahweh marked the lawn.

Then he remembered through mysterious sleep
The surgeon fingers probing at the bone,
The voice so far away, so rich and deep:
"It is not good for him to live alone."

Turning once more he found Man's counterpart
In tender parody breathing at his side.
He knew her at first sight, he knew by heart
Her allegory of sense unsatisfied.

The pawpaw drooped its golden breasts above
Less generous than the honey of her flesh;
The innocent sunlight showed the place of love;
The dew on its dark hairs winked crisp and fresh.

This plump gourd severed from his virile root,
She promised on the turf of Paradise
Delicious pulp of the forbidden fruit;
Sly as the snake she loosed her sinuous thighs,

And waking, smiled up at him from the grass;
Her breasts rose softly and he heard her sigh –
From all the beasts whose pleasant task it was
In Eden to increase and multiply

Adam had learned the jolly deed of kind:
He took her in his arms and there and then,
Like the clean beasts, embracing from behind,
Began in joy to found the breed of men.

Then from the spurt of seed within her broke
Her terrible and triumphant female cry,
Split upward by the sexual lightning stroke.
It was the beasts now who stood watching by:

The gravid elephant, the calving hind,
The breeding bitch, the she-ape big with young
Were the first gentle midwives of mankind;
The teeming lioness rasped her with her tongue;

The proud vicuña nuzzled her as she slept
Lax on the grass; and Adam watching too
Saw how her dumb breasts at their ripening wept,
The great pod of her belly swelled and grew,

And saw its water break, and saw, in fear,
Its quaking muscles in the act of birth,
Between her legs a pigmy face appear,
And the first murderer lay upon the earth.

Reprinted by permission of Carcanet Press from *Selected Poems*.

Alec Derwent Hope was born in 1907 (the same year as Auden and MacNeice) at Cooma, New South Wales. He is the Grand Old Man of Australian poetry. Educated at the University of Sydney and Oxford, he became a teacher and vocational psychologist and, later, Professor of English at the Australian National Universtity, Canberra.

PHILIP SALOM
FROM PRESERVATION: THINGS IN GLASS

A liquid prisoner pent in walls of glass – Shakespeare, 'Sonnet 5'

Hieronymus Bosch's choleric and full-of-dread
politics, the open-air pain-market under glass,

all things in aquariums, Orlan's latest operation
injecting lumps under her skin (after beauty, the beast)

(after the false spell, the false ruin) looking in the glass
like Photoshop. Small wizened Saints who are God's

front window, and in Otranto, in the cupboards,
in the boxes glassed in and misty, mouldy, but

not quite glue, the bones and stomachs of Italians
killed by Turks and kept as heroes, their pins loose

like a worn-out butterfly collection. And not
the grimmest synecdoches . . . This rest of us

after operations: the gut-worm they pulled out
with a pair of pliers and the man-who-was-host

now with a downward tilt of his eyebrows
while the worm's snug in a bottle of meths.

This him/us bent inside bottles like Houdini,
like Houdini's appendix, the biggest tooth-

fairy of them all failing to get him out.
"Whatever you say, don't say drowning."

The Scottish play, "break a leg" or "glacial"
not quite saying your lover's no good in bed,

preserved, the tangled fang we call wisdom
of restraint, along with tonsils, adenoids, bits of aint.

LOUIS ARMAND
PERPETUUM MOBILE

nuanced like afterthoughts
the delicate arrangement of the foreshore
in variegated shades
of complacency, other vagaries

curved glass & ticker tape
a panorama of statistics & difficult weather
forecast as far south as
van diemen's land

north to the arafura
a dark psychology
passed over in the official itineraries, except
for model cases

of rehabilitation an imaginary longitude
drawn between
the manifestly real & the unseen,
graphing probability

"high" or "low" fronts
focused on the screen
in gestural simulation tracing the onset of
instability

levelling out to an average far from the
epicentre,
miscegenated on the fringe
property rites

or stage directions for perpetual motion
describing
the evolution of this concept
in terms of political climatology,

inflation & the coming millennium
re. marx:
"the last phase of the universal historic form
is its comedy" . . .

but in the absence of
perspective, how flat everything appears
from the pre-
historic spars of manly ferries

ANDREW TAYLOR
SPRING

Spare, woody, rangy, scraggy, morose
these bushes solemn as Presbyterian
temperance weddings have suddenly thrown off
dark suits to dance in the bright wind
with undecorous brilliance – flesh pink
sexy purple, satiny seductive white
and scandalously passionate scarlet.

Where was it concealed, this riot and flamboyance
for the last nine months, this carnival
and brawl of colour?

In the dry limbs
of my unkillable Scottish forebears
(seven of whom lived beyond ninety)
in their thin frugal bodies, in their lean
faces and narrow minds, in the persistence
with which they fastened to unpromising soil
and flourished – was there a bud
of excess, a growth node of extravagance
a wee germ of triumphant indulgence
biding its time, as there is in the trees
and bushes they hacked out, nodding to me?

Hinterlands

TRACY RYAN ON POETS WHO SWITCH BETWEEN THE REGION AND THE WIDER WORLD

CAROLINE CADDY

Working Temples

Fremantle Arts Centre Press,
ISBN 1 863 68190 6

JEAN KENT

The Satin Bowerbird

Hale & Iremonger
ISBN 0 868 06640 0

ANTHONY LAWRENCE

New and Selected Poems

University of Queensland Press
ISBN 0 702 22980 6

JOHN BENNETT

Field Notes – Australia / Albion

Five Islands Press
ISBN 0 864 18551 0

CATHERINE BATESON

The Vigilant Heart

University of Queensland Press
ISBN 0 702 23048 0

MTC CRONIN

Everything Holy

Balcones International Press
ISBN 1 891 81104 5

EMMA LEW

The Wild Reply

Black Pepper
ISBN 1 876 04413 6

DENNIS HASKELL,

The Ghost Names Sing

Fremantle Arts Centre Press
ISBN 1 863 68199 X

IN THIS SELECTION of recent Australian titles there is a common ongoing concern with international interactions, whether through the poets publishing in journals in various countries, or through engagement at the level of subject matter. Whatever the Pauline Hanson mentality may declare, among poets the borders are open, if they were ever closed.

Working Temples is Caroline Caddy's sixth book of poems, most of which have been published by Fremantle Arts Centre Press – based in Western Australia, but with a national readership. In this volume Caddy demonstrates again the formal precision and vivid image-making for which she has become known. Caddy has long defied any simplistic notion of the "regional" that might once have been imposed on writers not issuing from the Sydney–Melbourne concentration – her previous book arose from a trip to Antarctica, and this one takes for most of its material a time spent in China. As if to counteract negative anticipation of tourist-snapshot poems, the book's blurb tells us Caddy's "longstanding interest in Asia and Asian cultures had its beginnings in the three years she spent in Japan as a child," as well as in more recent experiences of China.

There are poems like 'Tourism' that gesture consciously toward the problem of representing something traditionally seen as "other": "My pictures too are superimpositions / wanting to see this place / without the crowd / that gives its own absence / value". At points the book gives in to what seems like ready-made encoding too close to orientalist thinking for comfort. But at their keenest, the poems are charged with such physical presence – as in the oral encounter of 'Persimmon', or in the opening of 'March/Storm' ("Lightning explodes / as if it had been imbedded in the air") that the tricky business of rendering what Caddy calls the "hinterland", a "country where you don't speak the language", is more than mastered.

Caddy's volume includes poems translated into Chinese by Sharon Xiao Xia Jiang, upon which I cannot comment individually, since I don't read Chinese, or rather, can only "read" the poems in one of their potential functions for others like me: creating a sense of that "hinterland" which Caddy herself faced in the experiences that formed the poems, that sense of one's own "otherness".

By contrast, Jean Kent's third book of poems, *The Satin Bowerbird*, takes few risks, although it also deals in part with the ups and downs of living in another country, as signalled unsubtly by the cover image of a bowerbird superimposed on a shot of the Eiffel Tower! If Paris has frequently stood for an opposite pole or "cultured" metropolitan centre in antipodean binaries, we may expect to cover familiar territory here – "Where in this city could anything natural grow?" – or, as one of the other poems sums it up by title, 'Saos and Vegemite Beside the Seine'.

Here the issues of representation are less nuanced and the speaking voice less aware of them than in Caddy – how else could we find "in the Jardin des Plantes today, a giraffe- / tall black African / after a supermarket sortie" ('A Postcard to Paris'), at which point I'll stop quoting, reluctant to air the stereotype further.

Not all of Kent's material deals with the Paris sojourn, and there are better moments in poems like 'Between Wave Breaks at Watson's Bay', with its sharp evocation of a particular mother-daughter relationship (though this poem, like others, is marred by one bewilderingly over-alliterated line). 'The Humility of Poppy Buds' has some well-handled imagery, with blossoms "silkily unkinking" in a series of analogies, and generally an impressive sensitivity to detail. But what spoils many of the poems for me is their heavy-handedness. Those who like their poems sweet and soft will be less troubled by this book – Kent's work is usually well-received, and she has won several notable awards for previous writing. Ultimately it comes down to taste, and how hard-edged you like your poetry to be.

Sharper around the edges, and mostly without that "sweetness", but still in the realms of sensibility, are the *New and Selected Poems* of Anthony Lawrence. Anyone who missed the earlier volumes really will get the best of them here. Lawrence is widely-published and has also won many awards, some of his prize-winning work being included in this selection. For me his finest poems are the tight lyrics – "Fencing", for instance, from his very first book (though by no means the only phase in which he has produced these). This poem shows how he can convey something much larger through the colloquial and the understated-yet-graphic:

High tensile wire, when strained,

is a volatile thing.
I'd been warned how the wire can break,
whipping back through the eyes
of the fence posts, leaving your fingers
flexing at your feet, or worse,
your throat smiling redly from ear to ear.
You hear stories.

I was straining the last section before smoko.
I worked the handle of the strainer back and forth,
daydreaming, watching clouds move in.
Then I heard it: a loud ping like a struck tuning fork.
I leapt away from the fence as the wire
ripped past me – silver, on fire,
with my name cut into its tail.

But there are also very accomplished longer poems, such as 'Blood Oath', where that colloquial language is used to best effect. 'Blood Oath' too demonstrates Lawrence's capacity to assume personae – his characters' voices, whether here or in his many monologues, are always convincing. Sometimes the poems veer into overly romantic celebration or "self"-deprecation, but the selection on the whole contains his more muscular writing, particularly the poems that come to grips with the "natural" world.

John Bennett too is concerned with the "natural" world and its interaction with "culture", the possible tensions epitomised in one of the opening poems of his book, 'The Circumstance of Trees', where a friend walking among trees "is more interested in the fallen timber/imagining the raw wood feathering, sloughing/as he carves its meat down the grain". I say one of the opening poems because the book starts at either side, with *Field Notes Australia* on the one hand and on the other, *Field Notes Albion*, upside down – depending, of course, on which way you look at it! A gimmick perhaps, but one which does not detract from the actual reading. As we might guess, Bennett has divided his time, like his book, between the two hemispheres; born and raised in Britain but now resident in Australia, he has been an active organiser there for other poets and worked for a time with the National Parks and Wildlife Service. This experience must be what makes his poetry so alert to the physical environment; but Bennett is not simply a describer of place. He is interested in the difficult (hi)stories that place embodies – as in the long piece 'Surviving History' – and the discourses that underpin or overlay them – as in 'Landscape Proof', which runs extracts from public commentary on Lake Pedder alongside the poetic text. "What evidence can poets present a committee?", we are asked. If Bennett's diction is sometimes prosaic, this is often compensated for by the seriousness of intent and the acuteness of his imagery, not to mention the willingness to experiment, for example in 'A Platypus Inheritance', whose concrete-poem effect is sustained over thirteen pages in which "understanding emerges/from the shifting currents".

In the Albion section we tour the English and the Celtic, with an interesting though not, I suspect, fully exploited set of poems on the former spa town of Ilkley and its moorland, on through a Britain I (as an outsider) know instantly from its Tornado fighters "more ferocious than lightning" ('Welsh Pastoral'), and its "right of way" which "is English/with its own stile, breed of dog / and straight-forward approach / to the earth, 'not getting involved'" ('Eardstapa'). Bennett has attempted something intelligent and unusual with this book, and if it doesn't always "soar" as poetry but perhaps leaves us to complete the work, it nonetheless feeds the imagination and the conscience. My only gripe is the use throughout of a sans-serif font that makes reading so tiring over longer pieces.

Catherine Bateson's poems in her second full-length work, *The Vigilant Heart*, are situated in the social rather than the environmental. Her approach is simple – the standard free-verse lyric, sometimes in sequence – but her knowledges are complex, and grounded in the bodily-emotive rather than the cerebral. I mean these as descriptors without the negative value that is often ascribed to them. The simplicity is, in fact, deceptive. Bateson's poetry (and this was true too of her earlier volume, *Pomegranates from the Underworld*) reinserts into the public arena a kind of vision derived from specifically female experience – here especially the giving birth to and mothering of a child in danger of death. Some readers may find parts overly sentimental, in a soft-pedalled Sharon Olds mode; but to focus on the odd angel/heart/star pattern at the expense of the overall thrust is to miss the point. If some of the poems are perhaps ill-judged (I am thinking of, for instance, 'Prayer for the Dead: In memory of the victims of Port Arthur') there are many more whose truths must overcome the most cynical of readers. Bateson, like Anthony Lawrence in this one respect, has a great facility for the assumption of voices. It would be interesting to see

what she might do with radio drama or a verse play. She writes, too, with a keen awareness of the inadequacy of the role models offered to us as poets, whether in an affectionate nod to Bukowski from the depths of the domestic – "all those poems about drinking, screwing, fighting / – aren't they a bit personal – / a little trivial?" ('On Bukowski and Babies'), or as a rejection of the dead-end allowed to women poets:

If I'm called to give witness it's not to that –
death as a blanket, a comforter
but how life takes over, bustles in
opens the curtains,
gives the day a shake.
('Late Night Critique of Sexton and Plath')

Though the poems may be (unnecessarily) apologetic for their domestic scope – "I go only as far as is possible with two tired children" ('What I Do'), they are by no means ignorant of the social and political roles of women in building all sides of what we call "Australia":

My mouth full of words;
god and better, white and beast.
My heart decided, an obdurate muscle.
My finger on the trigger,
my poison in the waterhole.
Someone who looked like me, like you.
Someone signing our names.
('With What Intentions?')

The Vigilant Heart is a completely approachable book for all those who have known loss and responsibility, "for us all who have spat in death's eye/telling our birth stories" ('On Ward Seven West').

M. T. C. Cronin in *Everything Holy* has her variations on "birth stories" to tell, but they are unlike anyone else's narratives, and she is equally at ease looking death "in the eye". Philip Salom on the back cover speaks accurately of Cronin's "tough unsentimental lyrics" alongside her more meditative work, and poems like the title piece surely fit his first category:

I can see the ribs on the flesh
of his back
as he bends to set the clock

The execution of prisoners in China

is timed with the pre-operation prepping
of patients in Hong Kong
who are to receive their organs...

as does the 'The Sculptor', about a woman forming from mud the head of her dead brother:

Her fingers drawn together
cover his muddied eyes
Her fingers   recreate him
Nostrils sharp and bursting out
Cutting his outline
clear from the room
[...]
Hammer into that head
all that he forgets.

Cronin is unsentimental even when, or especially when, dealing with memory and trauma, as in her remarkable poem 'The Confetti Stone', more familiar in its formal approach than much of her work, but still unique in its intensity:

.   ..Someone – a girlfriend maybe

or her mother – had tried to convince her to have the
opal set
in a ring: like a memory in pride of place; like a black
eye mounted

on the back of her hand watching her from the
withered years,
crawled from its grave in the soil to watch her

as her father had done... And didn't just watch but
touched
with his prospecting fingers the body she will marry
tomorrow
under the marquee to another man.

Cronin is also at home with wry satire ('Eating Paint [after Anthony Lawrence]') that is never self-exempting; and in this book, as in her earlier work, unafraid to mine the corporeal for its subtlest as well as its grosser meanings – no mind/body split diminishes this poetry. Serious she may be, even deadly serious, but nonetheless sensual. Her bio-note tells us Cronin is a solicitor and researcher in feminist legal theory, and this is not tangential to the work. The book is modelled around a group of "law" poems that demonstrate her characteristically lateral and quirky way of thinking. These poems are

not "about" legal cases; rather their writer's immersion in that discourse has given her a particular understanding of how words structure perception; see for example her rendering of the duck "so represented that it could only be looking // for nothing restless nor anything / but a pencil drawing of the pale blue pond [...] for this contention I have the full support / of my subconscious not to mention//photographic proof" ('the law of ducks'). Cronin's hyperactive "subconscious" and peculiar ways with language continue with this book to take us into regions not so often touched upon in Australian poetry.

Emma Lew too moves in unaccustomed regions, as the haunting cover painting of her book *The Wild Reply* might indicate. That title can be read as description or sentence: her reply to poetic predecessors is unbroken-in, untamed by their conventions, and her voices are multiple, if insistent on certain themes. Lew possesses a freedom of diction reminiscent, if we must have predecessors, of Gig Ryan's, but all her own in style. She can be weirdly gothic ('The Recidivist', 'My Adventurer') and repetitively focussed on the narcotic, the opiate, the world of shadow – "shiver" is a signature word for Lew – or cuttingly terse – "Smile at me like you smile at police" ('Little Sister'), "...you can no more trick / the universe into granting favours / than your parents into loving you" ('Earlier Cartographers of the Moon') – almost in the manner of a John Forbes; or again a subtle evoker of sparse real and psychic landscapes ('Pond', 'Lumber'). Though her poems have been widely published in periodicals, this is Lew's first published collection, and it is exciting to find a first book that immediately strikes out in its own direction/s rather than playing it safe.

The poems in Dennis Haskell's collection *The Ghost Names Sing*, while perhaps "unobtrusive", as their blurb indicates, on the level of form, are nonetheless risk-taking in a different way: it is unfashionable in many quarters to take on an avowedly "spiritual" project, and for a (male) poet to make his speaking voices so nakedly vulnerable. I am thinking of poems like 'Recognition', addressed to one who has died of leukaemia, and of the gentle self-deprecation of poems like 'Natural Piety'. With all of Haskell's poems, no matter how small or apparently simple, there is a consciousness of the larger order (or disorder) of things, whether that be on a plane trip or at a funeral. He shuns the big effect for the meditative, the undervalued aspects of the domestic, and often for the satirical

('The Second Going', 'Australian Language's Tribute to the Times', and 'The Baked Style of Unemployment', a wry Aussie take on Yeats's Lake Isle). Opting for the lyrical in Haskell is not style-by-default, but an aesthetic choice – in 'Lineal Instinct', where the "honey-dew"-fed writer within the poem watches a swarm of bees and recalls "Plath's fuzzing, fetishistic poems", he muses, "Are they meant / to talk just to themselves?" – and though it is not a question Haskell answers in any absolute fashion, he reminds us in another context that the "cutting edge" may just leave us "[j]aggedly bleeding". Far from the stereotype of the sensitive "lyrical", reference-based poetry, Haskell's work never takes the "self" too seriously, but neither does it deny the self a place: his is a book for those who like their poetry with feeling that steers clear of the cloying.

Kristeva at the Ministry of Sound

by Robert Potts

JOHN TRANTER

Late Night Radio

Polygon, £7.95
ISBN 0 748 662383

Different Hands

Folio/Fremantle Arts Centre Press
ISBN 1 863 368241 1

CHRIS WALLACE-CRABBE

Whirling

Oxford Poets, £6.99
ISBN 0 192 888081 0

IN PREVIOUS CENTURIES, botanists would bring back the seeds, illustrations and pressed specimens of flora from far-flung margins of Empire; the stolen blueprints of paradisal gardens. With less sinister motives, it has been through anthologies that Australia's poetic flowerings have been brought to these shores: single volumes by most poets are still hard to find, with a few obvious exceptions, though the work of some publishers, Bloodaxe and Carcanet for example, has been laudable in ameliorating this situation.

It was through two anthologies, Peter Porter's *Oxford Book of Australian Verse* and Les Murray's *New Oxford Book of Australian Verse* that my own horizons were broadened. Both are edited by major international poets, and both men have a broad and passionate set of poetic sympathies. At the same time both highlighted, in their selections and in Porter's introduction, some of the battle lines that accompany the too-small world of poetry in any culture, and which are spot-lit in anthologising moments. As an outsider, I was (largely) immune to schism and sectarianism: the Melbourne-Sydney axis; the tensions between modernists and traditionalists; the choice of America or Europe or England as models. I found myself reading good, sometimes excellent, poems about different worlds, different lives. It is sometimes too easy to forget that this is one of the reasons we come to poetry in the first place.

One of the things that struck me was the peculiar speed with which Australian poetry had modernized itself, with the benefit of international models. Casting off an (unignorable) inferiority complex – the so-called "Cultural Cringe" – Australian poets seized on models from West Coast America, or the Beats, or European symbolists, or the English modernists such as Auden, in an attempt to throw off the Bush-oriented poetry that had dominated perhaps too long (and certainly long after most Australians were unequivocally urban-dwelling). It is an acceleration of cultural and political progress and burgeoning (if self-conscious) cultural confidence that Laurie Duggan amusingly ironizes in the short poem 'Australia':

I like the way we've
Been able to fuck things here
As good as anywhere else
In only half the time.

John Tranter, whose *Late Night Radio* is, astonishingly, his first full length collection to be published in this country, has been a seminal figure in this reorientation; the editor of a ground-breaking anthology, an influential stylist who emerged from the "generation of '68", and the editor of *Jacket*, a literary magazine on the internet, he is a postmodernist aware of his debts, whether to Ashbery and O'Hara or, further back, to Auden. So while this volume begins with two pieces of recognizably Australian pastoral – 'Backyard' and 'Country Vernada' – it isn't long before we are entering the slippery, sliding shifts of tone, register, diction and direction with which, despite that "postmodern" tag, we are perhaps too comfortable already.

What Tranter appends to these manoeuvres – almost stylistic tics, given how well-trodden the ground is – is a lively and engaging wit, on the one hand, and a self-conscious commentary on poetic process on the other. It's hard not to feel that the latter stems from a certain lack of confidence in the project: in his cinematic 'Those Gods Made Permanent', the longest piece in the collection, and a crucial one, Tranter writes

John Tranter

> ... we find the plot folding
>   up like a robot
> and stumbling off in the
>   wrong direction
> too abruptly for us to get our
>   bearings.
> Is this all the reward we are offered
> For our painstaking attention, for the strain
> Of our emotional investment? What we asked for
> Led to nothing, what we didn't want to see
> Was made plain.

In his descriptions preceding this (of plots and images from famous films, on the experience of watching the movies, on the nature of escapism and realism, on the way in which the flux of cinema – the rapid cuts and disjunctions – mirrors a modernist mediation of an incorrigibly various worlds), and in other poems, Tranter has offered just such a disorientation, raising exactly those questions of a reader's "investment" and "reward", and, I think, asking a necessary question as to whether such a balance-sheet approach to art and reception is valid. But here, as he refers to this process, he is being absolutely, pradoxically, perversely clear: Tranter, it could be argued, lacks faith in his audi-

ence, and grounds them with this reassuring explanation just as they threaten to get lost in the aesthetic he is describing.

Elsewhere, that aesthetic succeeds or fails in equal measure; Tranter, presumably, would argue that he is offering "open" poems which leave room for the reader to make sense and sensation as he or she will, and though this is as ever an impregnable position, it will always invite the question of how we might decide whether to come to Tranter's work for these purposes as opposed to anyone else's work, or, indeed, go to the movies instead.

Personally I enjoyed a number of these pieces, mainly for their humour and gentle sensitivity; and there are some excellent satirical swipes at anything from degrading late capitalism to suburban complacency, in which he is never less than sympathetic to the problems and complexities of his subjects. Where I became troubled was in the self-conscious references to exactly those questions of heritage and influence which, while articulating an Australian (though not exclusively Australian) "problem", are arguably of more interest to the poet than many of his putative readers.

For example, there is a suite of poems with titles like 'Leavis at the London Hotel', 'Sartre at Surfe's Paradise', 'Kristeva at the Ministry of Sound' (I made the last one up, but you get the idea), which jazzily imagine and reconfigure the inner lives of these critical icons, but freight the volume with a self-conscious weight of academe; the allusions – to Auden, say ("The apostrophe they invented / was easy to understand") or even The Battle of Maldon ("were ... [broken] ...") – are, partly, a levelling of the high and low cultural references that the book contains, but also a firming up of a place in a tradition; I was unconvinced of their purpose, and began to wonder how much one is supposed to have read already if one is to get the most out of Tranter's work. Ultimately, for all its pleasures (and there are many), this levelling is becoming commonplace; it is not asking new questions, it is not offering fresh pleasures, and it's hard not to feel that when you've read a few of these things, you've read them all.

Tranter's extra-poetic work, similarly, a selection of prose pieces called 'Different Hands', is an experimental work, denying authorial responsibility as far as possible. Using advanced computer software to reconstruct texts in terms of the frequency of their letter groups, Tranter produced, as he admits, "mostly dreck". He then improvised out of what little sense he found in the randomness, to form seven hybrid tales ('Lonely Chaps', for example, is an improbable blend of Radclyffe Hall and Biggles; and there is, admittedly, a neat skit on *Room With a View* in which the language of courtship and love is replaced by that of the property market). This is meant to distance us from authorial intention by letting these chance structures goven the creative process, but as Tranter has said elsewhere "the hand of the stylist – not to mention the theoretician – is always evident as it arranges the exhibits". Indeed, what he comes up with is material that oozes self-consciousness about the written word. One tires of writing that's about writing; one longs for the writing itself. And if some form of constraint is required, Tranter could do worse than consider some of the old-fashioned poetic forms (though I offer this fogeyish suggestion with my tongue partly in my cheek).

Chris Wallace-Crabbe

Chris Wallace-Crabbe is capable of the postmodern touches – there are elliptical shifts that surprise, and hazy ambiguities to play in. At times, he is asking the same questions as Tranter (and Ashbery) – when representing the world or one's thoughts and feelings, what do you include and what leave out? Is there even a possibility of adequate representation, and if not, how close can one come, and where does it fail? In his latest collection, *Whirling*, there is a prose poem, 'Snips of the Day', in which he asks "what would it be like to write a journal that managed to get everything in, which would flow and reach out sideways, forward and back, grasping the small and the large, all that myriad of impressions? … One needs a genre with appetite, with a huge belly, the kind of kaboodle Whitman had to invent for *Leaves of Grass*". What follows is a list of the quotidian, banal, topical, literary, philosophical, erotic and so on. One begins to understand an earlier line, on old age, that "it is time … perhaps to drop Russell and Rorty for Proust".

But Wallace-Crabbe is merely rehearsing an old poetic desire – a totalising, all-embracing representation – while gathering the fragments of memory and desire in appropriate celebration ("glorying" is a recurrent word) and elegy (his affecting description of bereavment: "the loss remains behind / Like never being well"). He too can mix his cultural registers; even on this topic, he remarks "Lendl said that after a match / he could remember every stroke. / I'll take that with a pillar of salt." There's also a delightful comic piece called "The Crims" on the romanticization of villains in Hollywood ("What has become of them, those actual gunmen, / Drily disguising the hurry / In which they live out chaotic combative lives, / Neither Bogart nor Peter Lorre?"). Wallace-Crabbe has not restricted himself to one line of enquiry.

Least successful, amidst this pleasant variousness, as he elegises not merely his own age and his losses but also the "dag-end" of the century, are the bland political statements. The anger is obvious, given that all attempts at style are suddenly junked, but "the usual dickhead political thugs", "the rule of local shitheads"and "sado-monetarism is hard to fit into a poem" are, perhaps, too bald, even when one recalls that Australia suffered the excesses of Reaganite-Thatcherite economic policy just like us.

But this is, on the whole, a beautiful volume, lively, alert, varied; and in its epiphanies it strives for a secular religiosity which in 'A Barbarian Catechism' and 'Near Arezzo' remind us that there is much to celebrate, and that art is still a means of so doing.

Opera of Atmospheres

by Kwame Dawes

MARK DOTY

Sweet Machine

Jonathan Cape, £8.00
ISBN 0 224 05119 9

MARK DOTY KNOWS he is being scrutinized. He knows that great things are expected of him. Michael Glover, quoted on the dust jacket of Doty's latest collection of poetry *Sweet Machine*, has declared Doty a veritable messiah of American poetry. "Why should we read Doty", he asks. The answer: "Because he is the finest American poet of the last twenty years", or since Lowell's death in 1977. The King died twenty years ago, long live the King. This is heady praise and the expectation is great. Doty seems unmoved by the pressure. In *Sweet Machine* he does what he has always done, write about what he cares about and in ways that he cares about. His verse almost seems determined not to sound like someone who thinks he is great. The tics of *Sweet Machine* become clear after reading a few poems – they are dogged tics, which may become classic Doty tics: the preoccupation with objects of art, the evocation of feeling, of sentiment, really, from a close study of objects; the use of questions (lots of questions); the preoccupation with light and gleam – with alchemy and its falsehood; and the much used by rarely explained notion of pouring. These are Doty tropes that recur again and again along with old themes of loss and a fascination with New York City. Tics are good sometimes; especially in the great poets: they are perfectly useful for imitators and saviours do need imitators.

But here, unlike in other collections, Doty seems self-conscious about his tics. He writes with wit about the implications of his capacity to extract from the objects of everyday life the conceits of human experience:

surfaces burnished
like a tidal stream
on which an excitation

of minnows boils
and blooms, artifice
made to show us

the lavish wardrobe
of things, the world's
glaze of appearances

worked into the thin
and gleaming stuff
of craft.

('Favrille')

Indeed, much of Doty's poetry represents a fascinating assortment of objects transformed into moments of lyrical reflection. The system is almost predictable and his first lines so often have a syntactic uniformity that one is forced to regard what he does as tantamount to the rhetoric of form: "Sleeves of oyster, smoke and pearl, / linings patterned with chrysanthemum flurries" ('White Kimono'); "Fog-lacquered, / varnished in thin / pearl glaze" ('Fog Suite'); "bureaus angled like ziggurats, / round mirrored vanities in African veneers" ('Emerald'); "Toxic salts, arsenic and copper, / metal oxides firing the glassmaker's slag" (Murano'); and there are more. It is the cadence, yes, but there is also the pattern of the verse's outworking – the movement from the object, that still thing, that he alchemizes into something gleaming, something brilliant by the sheer grace of his language, and that he then finds, through a remarkable act of poetic acrobatics, some profound human meaning to hang the image upon.

Doty does all this well, because he is a stunning craftsman. Yet one senses in Doty, a certain slag, an unusually present preoccupation with the business of writing. Now it is true that all poetry is, in some way, about writing of poetry; but the wiser poets have learned to disguise this self-indulgence with the wonderful tools of detachment and masking. Doty does not relish masks, and so his confessional in *Sweet Machine* turns out to be a confession of his own concerns as a writer, his own uncertain intimations of the business of making art.

And this is what leads to the second tic of these poems. Questions. Doty is constantly questioning. Now, I don't think his questions are anything but rhetorical, but he turns to these rhetorical questions with uncanny regularity, to the extent that we begin to wonder what he wants to nail down, if anything at all. On one hand, the effect of these questions is to create a casual conversationality about the verse that is not just pleasant, but actually quite engaging. But it must be there for a reason – the questioning, I mean, mustn't it? In the elegant poem of loss and re-memory 'Lost Kimono' presents us with the first question. It is rhetorical, but it may well have stood (and offered a quality of sage-like brilliance to Doty) were it offered as a statement: "Doesn't rain make a memory more intimate?" he asks. It does, one is willing to believe. Would the line have suffered from the stating of it: "rain makes a memory more intimate"? Again and again, Doty presents us with these "truths" these intimations of truth in the form of questions. But questions are what this self-reflexivity about writing is all about. Indeed, the most explicit poem about writing, 'Lilies in New York' is basically a grand question about the motivations of the artist, the choices an artist makes and the meaning of the artifact; in this instance, an unfinished line drawing. The questions work well here – they allow us to unveil the mechanics of the poet – the tricks that the poet uses, the value of the poem at the end of the day.

> Is it that
> He wants us to think, This is a drawing
> Not a flower and so reminds us
>
> That the power of his illusion,
> Alive below the lily's neck,
> Is trickery? A formal joke,

You can understand here why Doty is so highly praised: he is smart, and his ability to conflate this exploration of the motive behind a poor drawing, or a sketchy drawing represents a moment of poetic brilliance. The problem, though, is that we are left wondering if all of Doty's poems are, indeed, a joke – a formal joke. That would not be so bad in itself, especially if we relish the game of entering into his joke every time; but the problem with jokes is that if the same trick is used again and again, we grow weary of the joke – it loses something in the rehearsing. What is most rewarding about this aspect of Doty's collection, however, is that we get an insight into Doty's craft, and he dares us to know this and still not be impressed by the magic he manages nonetheless.

In two poems which would appear testy were they not as funny as they are Doty is willing to laugh at himself, at his tics, and to, at the same time, take on the critics of his verse, of his affectations, if you will. In the first 'Concerning Some Recent Criticism of His Work', he uses a deftly handled ditty and wonderful throw up of his gayness to snub his nose at the critics:

> – Glaze and shimmer
> lustre and gleam,
> can't he think of anything
> but all that sheen?
>
> – No such thing,
> the queen said,
> as too many sequins

In the second 'Concerning Some Recent Criticism of His Work', he takes the critic more seriously and in the process provides us with a Doty manifesto that could, one imagines, become the mantra for a movement of his making:

> What else to do
> with what you adore
>
> but build a replica?
> My model theatre's
>
> an opera of atmospheres:
>
> what's the world but shine
> and seem?

Of course, Doty's work, while fascinated by elements of light and the way light only suggests beauty ('Murano' is a remarkable orgy of light imagery rooted in an uncanny fascination with glass and Italian craft) is not all light. The latter part of the book offers some of the better poems in this collection – poems that show Doty in a most reflective and ingenuous mood.

His homage to James Merril in 'Thirty Delft Tiles' shows what he can do with a tea cup and history. In 'The Embrace' Doty returns to an important theme of his earlier work – the stark meaning of death and loss, and he approaches the theme with the nakedness of a simple lyric, a narrative that seeks its magic in the moment he is describing – the apparition of a long dead friend. These are rich poems of confidence and grace. 'Tatoo' is one of my favourites for here Doty does his alchemy – from object to moment, and he manages to segue into the conceit of the poet being a skein of skin to be written upon. It is daring, and deftly managed.

The tightrope walk works here. It does not always end in triumph. But the collection ends with at least two triumphant poems, triumphant for their ability to find moments of gleaming and light in the business of anthems. The title poem 'Sweet Machine' is a strange tale that is uncertain about whether to be erotic or not, that almost drains a moment of its sociological and political meaning to find the poem. And in that there is something New York and disturbing about the moment.

Significantly, the collection's penultimate piece 'Mercy on Broadway' is an anthem to Broadway that is so heavily weighed by pathos and tragedy that it seems unlikely that he will manage to give it wings, give it "gleam", if you will. But he does. Broadway is the thing in this piece, and the thing is resonant with meaning:

> ... I looked into the shiny cup
> of ambulant green and I thought
>
> Somebody's going to live through this.
> Suppose it's you? Whatever happens to me,
>
> to us, somebody's going to ride out
> These blasted years, somebody if I'm still lucky

years from now will read this poem and walk on Broadway. Broadway's not one,

> and Broadway lasts. Here the new
> hat, the silhouette of the hour.

Doty is entering the familiar space of poets who intimate on mortality and what he offers here is no different, in essence, from a Shakespearean sonnet on beauty, or a Keatsian ode to the eternal. Doty's nightmare, however, is palpable – there is this quality of death, the echo of the coughing of men and women suffering from terminal diseases, young men and women, that hangs over all these poems. And it is because we know this, because we know that Doty is still mourning each day, that we understand the grace caught in a poem like 'Mercy on Broadway'.

Maybe Doty is becoming quite readable and predictable, but there is something comforting in knowing that he knows what he is doing and continues to do it because he likes to do it that way. And it ain't half bad. As for his second career as poetry's messiah, he is, gratefully, unimpressed with the hype. He knows that in verse messiahs are safely crowned only after they are dead and gone.

Virtuous Travel

by William Scammell

MICHAEL SCHMIDT

Lives of the Poets

Weidenfeld & Nicolson, £22
ISBN 0 297 84014 2

MICHAEL SCHMIDT'S WORKLOAD is the eighth wonder of the literary world. Poet, novelist, reviewer, publisher, editor, translator, lecturer, publicist, broadcaster, correspondent, committee man, pillar of the arts; more English than the English yet open to every culture under the sun, his prodigious output makes Hercules look like a slacker, issuing in more words a month than the average scribbler's yearly haul. When the IRA blew up his whole Manchester operation he was back in

business, smiling, before you could say Sir Arthur Quiller-Couch then hey presto here's this 850-page tome telling us all about ourselves from Richard Rolle of Hampole to the day before yesterday and taking in almost every poet of note inbetween.

It starts with a little set-piece in a Dublin studio. Brodsky, Walcott, Heaney and Les Murray are gathered round a table to discuss poetry, politics and language, with Schmidt in the chair. Sounds promising, until the thumbnail sketches of the poets and their background arrives, and some ponderous truisms. ("It is one of the poet's tasks to listen and transcribe".) The putative subject of this opening fanfare is the deregulation of the muses, postcolonialism, the empowerment of new voices, but you can tell that Schmidt's heart isn't really in these fashionable platitudes. Those who have read his previous critical books, and winced their way through the editorials in PN Review, will soon find themselves on familiar ground.

Schmidt's big problem, or one of them, is C. H. Sisson, whom he mistakes for another Eliot, as does, perhaps, the poet himself. Sisson adopted all the mannerisms and reactionariness of the aged eagle, but without possessing any of the saving genius: depth of feeling, extraordinary discrimination and sensibility, an intellect that could see through almost all the varieties of literary posturing at a thousand yards. A second problem for Schmidt was Donald Davie, who chose to be an academic first and a poet second, and who supposed that adversarialism could supply whatever it is that fuels an Auden, Hughes, Lowell or singer of modern hymns. All this means that Schmidt is too taken up with his skirmishes against received opinion, too anxious to duff up whatever is deemed glib, metropolitan, Faberish, overpraised, too buffeted by the mandarin tones of Academe, whose confidence in its own priestly discourse is so often misplaced.

After the opening disappointments, and silly hope that Schmidt had been born again as an illuminator rather than a categoriser, I looked up two or three areas in which I have delved myself. Keith Douglas is singled out for special treatment in the chapter on the Second World War poets, rightly, but the discussion rambles all over the place, seldom alighting on the best things in his poems. Rosenberg is mentioned for comparative purposes, again rightly, but then so are Edward Thomas and Ivor Gurney, who are utterly and completely different in kind. Alun Lewis, "wonderful in patches", is not discussed at all. Instead we get A. D. Hope, Randall Jarrell, Norman MacCaig and Edwin Morgan, as though they had something in common. That leaves out of account most of the British and American poets who wrote about the war, and drags in some for whom it is an irrelevance.

Back to Eliot. Here Schmidt has an interesting big stick to cudgel us with:

Eliot's poetry has a comparable importance within the tradition to Dryden's and Wordsworth's in earlier centuries, effecting a renewal in poetic language. Even today 'Prufrock' and The Waste Land are more challenging and 'contemporary' than much work produced last year or last decade. They are contemporary, present in the way great poetry remains and available, entering our aural memory and there. It is with Eliot and Pound that our poetic and critical language, our sensibility, are thoroughly shaken out. If the dust has settled again, if the challenge of Modernism has not been accepted in the longer term, it is our loss. Against the formal rigour and wholeness of Eliot's oeuvre the fiddlings of post-Modernism have a facile and fudged look. The cold

hand of convention grips firmly; those radical intelligences which turn our eye back to the informing tradition and help us to pry ourselves free are few.

That's well said, or at least still needs saying, despite the sludgy, schoolmasterish prose and the second-hand vocabulary. I'm not so sure about the "challenge of Modernism" having been refused, though I know it's a standard debating point. That particular battle of the books, spurred on by bystanders like Alvarez and Edna Longley, is surely over. The only challenge that matters is to write well, whether like Hughes or early Fenton or Muldoon, none of whom was untouched by Modernism. The notion that one ought to stand within calibrating distance of 'Marina', 'Rhapsody on a Windy Night' or 'Hugh Selwyn Mauberley' is simply barium meal for the seminar group.

If comprehensiveness is a virtue – 250 poets or more set in their times and places, with "influences" traced and judgements peppering out like buckshot – then this is a virtuous trawl through all the big and little fish that swim in metre, and deviations therefrom. Given what goes on in a thousand writers' groups, the hubris implicit in all those poetry "masterclasses" taught by incompetents, the democratic rush to bogus prizes and poetry polls, the urge to spread a little art over the halt, the dying and the maimed in lieu of redistributive taxes, this book at least takes its subject seriously, and can be recommended on that ground alone. Hands up those who can discuss Drayton's *Polyolbion*, have dipped into Landor or Canon Dixon or Burns Singer, or reeled away from John Riley and Veronica Forrest-Thomson?

I bought Schmidt's *50 Modern Poets* and its American follow-up and then gave them away because they were so boring. I shan't give *Lives of the Poets* away since it is at least a useful reference guide to names and dates. Frederic Raphael thought it worthy of its Johnsonian title. I don't. The recipe is biographical vignette plus some confident-sounding analysis which has a wonderful way of missing the point. E.g. "the failure of *Samson Agonistes*", or "Expression exceeds occasion in *Paradise Lost*". (Milton as a graveyard for critics. Discuss.) Or: Lawrence and Hughes "could hardly be more different in their tonalities and in their moral vision". Or: Edgell Rickword's 'To the Wife of a Non-Interventionist Statesman' as "brilliant, rough-cast rhetoric", when it's precisely the neo-Augustan smoothness that threatens to undermine its anger.

Or: Craig Raine's verse as "missing...human impulse", "the product of leisure and tedium". Raine still rankles, evidently, in Schmidt's demonology, for having grabbed the headlines and advances. That slot is now occupied by Simon Armitage, "acclaimed with the same over-emphasis as Raine was in the 1980s... It is not impossible that they Armitage and Duffy may raise the audience with them".

That is the audience of writer-reader-listeners. To be raised up with Schmidt, however, is a dubious honour – the elitist sniff coupled with a tin ear. I prefer my elitism straightforwardly Eliotic, Audenesque, Hughesian, O'Brienistic, with some consonance between the pepper and salt of work accomplished and insights secured.

Plain Speaking

by John Greening

PETER BLAND

Selected Poems

Carcanet, £9.95
ISBN 1 85754 357 2

ALTHOUGH HE IS now in his sixties, Peter Bland is not very well known in this country, and this new volume from Carcanet gathers together work from at least half a dozen earlier publications. His relative anonymity over here is a result of a life spent wandering between two worlds, or three if we count the world of the stage, where he has made his living. Born in Scarborough, he emigrated to New Zealand at the age of twenty and has since shuttled between England and the antipodes with substantial periods in each. This affects the structure of this book, which begins with 'The Old Country' and then proceeds to swing back and forth, twenty pages or so at a time. The last and most recent section has the general title 'Embarkations' and this continues the restless alternating motion. This should create a fruitful tension, and this book has all the potential for a really gripping collection, but I am afraid that I found it disappointingly vapid and repetitive.

His favourite manner is a puzzled innocence, which sounds phoney to me, like the adopted tone of an adult talking for the benefit of children. I lost count of the times I came across – "How that frail bridge shook as we crossed" or "How / elegant the generals' wives are" or "How I love this place where earth and water meet"... Peter Bland has made his living as an actor, and there is just something "put on" in this poetry, reflected in certain stylistic affectations (i.e. poising "it's" or "each" or "an" at the end of a line). He likes monologues, and has written in *PN Review* that he has turned increasingly to that form. Yet his sequence about Crusoe is a poor thing by comparison with the late Iain Crichton Smith's or Elizabeth Bishop's. In fact, it finds him leaning more heavily than ever on cliché in an attempt to sound colloquial: "Offers from a brothel in The Shambles / I turned down flat. My 'pet slave'/was all the rage..."

But my most serious doubts about these poems concern the lack of a charge in the diction, and they bring to mind again some words of Iain Crichton Smith's that what our poetry needs "is a new music. Not a new imagery, but a new music". There have been plenty of "primitives" in verse, the best of them combining narrative and drama with at least some feeling for the music – one thinks of the American Philip Levine, or even Bland's one-time compatriot James K. Baxter. But a glance at Baxter's work, say 'The Cold Hub' reminds us what poetry is. Bland seldom plays with words, rejoices in words, or if he does, the results are dubious ("In a Peasholm park paddle-boat / kids play pirates"): he does not seem to want us to ponder their sound, their wider resonance. The greatest poetry is plain, I have no doubt, and we know what Heaney meant when he said his own early work was stained glass and he wanted to write like window glass. But it's very hard to achieve and – like that wondrous cloth spun for the Emperor – very easy to persuade yourself you are looking at it. Allen Curnow, from whom Bland has learnt some mannerisms, such as the use of quotations within a poem, manages to be at once simple, colloquial, witty and magnetically profound, like the best Metaphysical poetry. Although Bland offers plenty of humour (one of his strengths) there is nothing of the Metaphysical about him – his attempts at striking imagery often end as bathos ("grief quickens them / like a cup of tea") and indeed, one feels that his reaction to such a style might be how he reacts to beached whales "as bits of the dark, left over, midnight / ocean offal, or pieces of a black / horizon to be booted". He boots a lot, as did his friend James Baxter, but they are in different leagues. Bland's voice seems to come from the sixties, via Chuang Tzu and Lao Tsu, wonderful writers but dangerous models. There is a terse quality to some of his work, with its bare end-stopped lines, that is very Chinese. His themes, too, are reminiscent of Tu Fu, the greatest poet of exile (perhaps he knows those excellent versions made by another New Zealander, Rewi Alley). The best of this book shifts genially between image and idea ('Trains' is finely achieved, and the sequences dedicated to Louis Johnson, which combine many of his preoccupations) and while I welcome Carcanet's generosity to a neglected poet, I cannot recommend a poetry that is deaf to the wild calls and tidal tensions that should feed it.

Simple Gifts

by Neil Powell

WILLIAM SCAMMELL

All Set to Fall Off the Edge of the World

Flambard, £6.95
ISBN 1 873226292

THESE ARE DIFFICULT days for the non-metropolitan poet who wants to stay in touch with urban life, in which the intuitive pull of landscape and the glitzy quick-wittedness of the city seem harder than ever to reconcile. The rapt wonder with which the country mouse traditionally regards his cousin from town is increasingly displaced by fearful incomprehension.

In his last collection, *Five Easy Pieces* (1993), William Scammell had a brave stab at bridging this gap; but in *All Set to Fall Off the Edge of the World*, he seems tacitly to admit that it may, after all, be unbridgeable. The new book is divided into three sections 'Back of Beyond', 'Barnacle Bill', 'Lost and Found', of which the first, in which the poems are mostly rooted in his Cumbrian landscape, seems to me much the most successful. Here, Scammell's easy familiarity with his subjects, far from dimming his perception, guides him effortlessly (or so it seems) to the tellingly exact epithet: in 'The Tryout', for instance, the done-to-death subject of a ruined churchyard is brought into perfect focus by such details as "gate pillars ... fallen down / and comfortable in the grass" and "stones... humble enough to let / me play at Stonehenge with them", where "comfortable" and "humble" gentle insist on an intimacy both of scale and of relationship; "this",

says Scammell, "is how time / grazes the conscious mind". The sense of country things being at once contemporary and timeless recurs elsewhere – "big drums of straw" are "newfangled yet ancient" - while an abandoned farmyard provides further instances of objects which have achieved an honourable state of decaying repose: the harrow is "rusty and fast asleep" and "even the skip /needs another skip to haul it away". He is good, too, on animals: a stretched-out cat with "paws fore and aft / like a gunboat" is vivid and startlingly right, though blackbirds bounding "over the lawn like animated teapots" risks quaintness. These poems share an affectionate engagement which only a town mouse would mistake for sentimentality.

The central sequence is attractive too, if not quite such an unqualified success: Scammell's Barnacle Bill is more of a generalised Everyman, a character to whom universally recognisable things happen, than a pungently individual Ancient Mariner. The result is a slight sense of emptiness at the centre of the poems, though the surrounding dobber of the seafarer's life is described with typical accuracy and relish:

All the seamen's missions had a ping-pong table,
a dartboard, thick china mugs and a desperate
collection of paperbacks printed on yellow paper
that held smudges in perpetuity, including
most of the geometrical solids and the mortal
remains of many small wings and mandibles.

It's a lovingly assembled rag-bag, and so indeed is the book's final section, which unashamedly collects poems which simply wouldn't fit elsewhere. Scammell's comments on political or cultural matters usually command ready assent "It's 'The Angel of the North' versus / minimalist conceptualisations", he writes, in a piece lamenting the death of public sculpture — even when they seem, as there, a shade too bluntly stated. More oblique, and the better for it, is 'Not Reaching Ireland', where he admits to possessing "more than a hint of the brass neck / the English hide away in their three-piece suits/and four-piece grammar". Of the others, I particularly liked 'The Party', a thank-you poem for an evening of good food, drink and company – a piece which seems to glance over its shoulder towards the celebrations of civilised pleasures and simple gifts in Ben Jonson, whose gruff generosity of spirit has much in common with Scammell's.

Home and Colonial

by Paul Groves

JON STALLWORTHY

Rounding the Horn: Collected Poems

Carcanet, £14.95
ISBN 1 85754 163 4

WHERE DOES JON Stallworthy belong? His forebears rode the tide of history between Preston Bissett, Buckinghamshire, and the antipodes. His *Collected Poems* contains a family tree whose declared roots are John (d. 1744) and Ann (d. 1771) and whose branches extend down eight generations to the poet's three children. His wife Jill Waldock (b. 1938) is mentioned just once, as the dedicatee of 'Making a Bed' (inexplicably left out of the Contents); while his son Jonathan (b. 1965) is referred to movingly in 'The Almond Tree': the expectant father arrives at the maternity hospital only to be told by a doctor 'your son is a mongol'. Incidentally, 'The Almond Tree Revisited' appeared in Stallworthy's 1974 volume, 'The Almond Tree' in his 1978, a perplexing back-to-frontness.

For many readers, his first appearance was on the cover of Jeremy Robson's *The Young British Poets* (1972). There he is, handsome, tousled, smiling boyishly between a cherubic Brian Patten and a darkly serious Dom Moraes. In Al Alvarez's *The New Poetry* of a decade earlier he is nowhere to be seen. John Fuller, the younger by two years, makes it into both and has to this day the stronger reputation. Will *Rounding the Horn* (he was conceived in New Zealand and born in Great Britain following a lengthy passage aboard a rusty freighter) challenge that? It is doubtful, as – for all his humane graces – Stallworthy is the more constricted poet. Both are, of course, solidly upper-middle-class: Fuller's father became a director of the Woolwich Building Society, Stallworthy's was Nuffield Professor of Obstetrics at Oxford University; Fuller *fils* attended St Paul's School and did national service in the RAF, Stallworthy attended the Dragon School and Rugby, beginning his army service in 1953 and serving in the Royal West African Frontier Force. Appearing simultaneously with the Collected Poems is Stallworthy's autobiography *Singing School*.

I would urge you to look at both. The *Collected Poems*, for all its 230-odd pages, prompts questions that it alone cannot satisfy. It starts with *The Astronomy of Love* (1961) and ends with *The Guest From The Future* (1995). The intervening span sees Stallworthy developing little in his range and voice, simply because his early work was so mature and assured. As a seven-year-old he knew that what he wanted to do with his life was write poems; and those he has written have been unvaryingly precise and poised. He abjures free verse, and rhymes with such dogged conviction as to cock a snook at the experimenters and pluralists of the last thirty years. He will have no truck with trends and trendies: his vision is steadfast and somewhat old-fashioned. 'A poem about Poems About Vietnam' excoriates the ranters and posturers of the sixties; I do not suppose that, even now, his exact contemporary Michael Horovitz and he would make harmonious dinner-party guests.

Stallworthy is a trustee of the Wilfred Owen estate and has edited his poems. This led to a noted literary controversy with Jon Silkin in the mid-eighties over breach of copyright regarding the latter's edition of Owen's verse. Stallworthy, in *The Times Literary Supplement*, described himself as Silkin's friend but the dour northerner would have none of it. Despite his rugged *Boy's Own* image (for three years he represented Oxford at rugby, but never got a 'blue'), Stallworthy comes across as a gentleman – indeed, a gentle man. The derring-do of his early verse never completely deserts him yet is tempered by tenderness, especially in *Hand in Hand* (1974). This contains some of the best love poems you will encounter anywhere: discreet, sincere, and for the most part unsentimental. Sometimes his honesty can court embarrassment: in 'Positives' we learn of soured romance:

> Nothing of our love lives –
> the children you wanted
> lie locked in my scrotum

This is a rare slide towards risibility; the amount of tonal slippage in the book is surprisingly small.

There is enough high-quality verse in this volume to ensure that he will bring quiet delight to readers for years to come. He sends neither himself nor others up, and is blissfully – or disturbingly – free of irony. Humour is largely absent. Craftsmanship is all. He turns out poem after poem like a cabinetmaker perfecting dovetail or tongue-and-groove and French-polishing everything to a high shine. The last pieces here are synthetically bright; since his talents are not best suited to the extended poem, the effort of creation can unflatteringly show. Although he is a wordsmith par excellence, in the long 'The Guest from the Future' words outpace meaning with unsettling exuberance.

His technical virtuosity is impressive. The only error I spotted was in 'You not with Me': the scheme falters in stanza four when he tries to rhyme "world" with "thrown". His original choice must have been 'hurled' and should be reinstated. He shares affinities with those poets represented in Robert Conquest's *New Lines* anthology of 1956 in his appetite for clarity, sobriety, and order. Reading this book is like judging a competition where most poems deserve to be short-listed and many deserve to win. The numerous successes include 'Sindhi Woman', 'Quiet Wedding', 'Feet off the Ground', 'Green Thought', 'The Postman', 'An Evening Walk', 'Firstborn', 'Message Received', 'African Violets', and 'The Play of Hands'. However, 'Old Flames' (about the burning of billets-doux) reads like ardent juvenilia; 'A Proposal' is oddly naive; 'At St Gennys' sounds like something published in 1956 rather than 1986; and 'The Girl from Zlot' is a victim of its own cleverness and artificiality. This is comfortable North Oxford poetry, hardly reflecting raw experience, and miles from the world of needle-strewn underpasses and premillennial soup kitchens.

All told, the book marks a real achievement. Eleven poems start with 'Dear' or 'My dear' and one is reminded of Larkin s final line in 'An Arundel Tomb' – 'What will survive of us is love' – when Stallworthy writes:

> I answer that my poems all
> are woven out of love's loose ends;
> for myself and for my friends.

Singing School: The Making of a Poet, John Murray £16.99
ISBN 0 7195 5715 1

KATE CLANCHY
WHEN MY GRANDMOTHER SAID
SHE SHOULD NEVER HAVE LEFT

New Zealand, land of her birth,
breakfast lamb-chops,
and frequent, casual earthquakes,
it frightened us.
To cast her net so very wide
over years, decades, lives –
was like a ground tremor starting,
spreading quick as misgivings,
wrinkling oceans, rumpling borders,
spiralling out of the Southern hemisphere
to compass Moscow and the War,
lap at England, Hampshire, here.

And then to let the sonar rings
reach our feet and pass us,
loop us, to pull them back
with that single gesture,
uptailing me, my cousins, brother,
into new volcanic fissures,
dowsing my father, uncle, aunt
in the China Sea till they paled to thoughts;
letting all our books and paintings
bob to other hands, like jetsam,
to push even my grandfather under
with his Captain's hat, his careful letters;
to furl all this in her fist at the epicentre,
where she stood, fifteen,
a skinny, straight-browed girl,
waiting for plates to settle flat
on the dresser, her cup
to click in the dent in the saucer,
the framed map of the Empire
to sway back horizontal,
for everything to be
as if nothing had happened,
and then to toss the twisted paper
in the grate to light a fire, later –

that shook me.

E. A. MARKHAM
THE HUSBANDS

Tonight, he will talk of the rivers
Of the world, quoting old Mitterrand; and I
Will counter with churches, Cathedrals, mosques. This jabbing

At torso with a fist of speech triggers commentary
By partners off-stage, tired of blood-sports. They
Have already thrown in the towel:
What's to be learnt from this but who controls

The vocabulary when the story is next told?
We agree, don't we, that partners are the travel-companions
We love best, when they adopt us as strangers humouring

Our foibles. (The day she was Cleopatra, kind to her bargeman.
And then Liz to his Richard gigoling down the Rhine.
Me too: she was with me last year in Umbria

(No shortage of placenames to frolic) at the Temple
Of SANTA MARIA DELLA CONSOLAZIONE:
I blasphemed her Pope's right boot proffered
To be kissed to a dazzle of silver, which is her due.)

Ah, the acts of omission that divide us. So we fault
The map of countries not discovered, and hint at dialogue
With the cartographer who thinks we're too old to travel.

And the talk amongst ourselves meanders past river
And Tabernacle to remembered scenes of the children
On holiday playing near a pool and painting the world crayon.

That's cool, you know, like who ate well in Vilnius, Lithuania
Or in Shanghai before the burgers moved in. And did you know
That the Ristorante Mino on the Via Magenta in Roma
Is the worst hole in the universe? Ah,

By morning, bless you, our friends all fit the vocabulary
Of blame; images of dough rising like sex, yeast
Us through the night, new bread for partners
Who think they know all about breakfast.

NEWS/COMMENT

NET VERSE

A LOT OF good Australian writers have latched onto the Internet; I've already mentioned some of them in this column. A good place to look for others is the Australian Writers on Line site at **http://www.ozemail.com.au/~awol/home.htm** with its many links to web journals and home pages. Another huge resource, which appears to list every Australian who's written anything at all, is *Ozlit* at **http://www.ozlit.org** This also has book announcements, competitions and many other resources.

Among the many sites maintained by individual poets, a few that stand out are Andrew Burke's at **http://www.bam.com.au/andrew/** the surreal **http://postbox.library.usyd.edu.au/~pbrown/** of Pam Brown, and Alison Croggon's excellent one at **http://www.fortunecity.com/victorian/bronte/338/**. All these have admirably simple, fast-loading layouts. They're easy to read, and give enough samples of each poet's work to enable you to decide whether you want to buy the books.

Alison is also the editor of *Masthead*, an Australian print journal which archives its past issues complete at **http://www.geocities.com/SoHo/Studios/5662/** Only the first edition (well worth a browse) is available as I write, though the second might also be there by the time you read this.

Its print roots anchor *Masthead* more firmly in Australia than is possible for entirely Web-based journals. Whether this is an advantage, a disadvantage, or just a difference depends on your point of view. Thus there's a strong internationalist flavour to the online *Jacket* at **http://www.jacket.zip.com.au/** In five editions, John Tranter has managed to establish an enviable reputation for it as one of the best literary journals of the genre. Another excellent journal has recently changed its location on the Web. *The Animist* can now be found at **http://theanimist.netgazer.net.au** and includes multimedia works using MIDI and RealAudio as well as more conventional poetry and articles.

Send any good links from any part of the planet to **peter@hphoward.demon.co.uk**

EDITORS
Michael Hulse and John Kinsella

FOUNDING EDITOR
Jon Silkin (1930–1997)

EDITORIAL ASSISTANT
Helen Richman

EDITORIAL OFFICE
School of English
University of Leeds, Leeds LS2 9JT
PHONE: +44 (0) 113 233 4794
FAX: +44 (0) 113 233 4791
EMAIL: stand@english.novell.leeds.ac.uk
WEBSITE: http://saturn.vcu.edu/~dlatane/
stand.html

RICHMOND OFFICE
David Latané
Department of English, VCU
Richmond, VA 23284-2005, USA
EMAIL: dlatane@vcu.edu

PERTH OFFICE
Clive Newman
PO Box 2112, Kardinya
Western Australia 6163
PHONE/FAX: 00 61 8 9331 1015
EMAIL: cnewman@iinet.net.au

SUBSCRIPTIONS AND
COMPETITIONS
Linda Goldsmith
Haltwhistle House, George Street
Newcastle upon Tyne NE4 7JL
PHONE: +44 (0) 191 273 3280
FAX: +44 (0) 191 272 0040

Subscriptions:
Four issues
£16.00 (UK) £18.00/US$29.00 (overseas)
Unwaged/student:
£10.00 (UK) £12.00/US$22.50 (overseas)
Single copy:
£4.75 (UK) £5.75/US$11.00 (overseas)

Stand MAGAZINE

NEW SERIES   VOLUME I   NUMBER I   MARCH 1999

Men and Women
Water
Representations
Anthony Hecht
Olygoptl

£4.75 / $11.00

*In this issue: fiction by Keith Botsford, Christopher Hope
and Jane Stevenson; poetry by Harry Clifton, David Harsent,
Tracey Herd, Les Murray, Ruth Padel, Peter Redgrove,
Penelope Shuttle, Elizabeth Smither, Pauline Stainer,
Jon Stallworthy and John Hartley Williams; Anthony Hecht
in interview; and much more.*

Hugh Buchanan, *A Gathering Breeze* (1998, acrylic and oil, 112 x 81 cm).
Courtesy of the artist and the Francis Kyle Gallery, London W1.

EVA SALZMAN

TO OXFORD UNIVERSITY PRESS, IN HOSPITAL

As befits an afflicted poet
nearing an operative time,
I lay in the ward Robert Bridges
– who was doctor of men and of rhyme.

Nearby hung poetic displays
of the Laureate's history at Bart's.
(My surgeon was moved to comparisons
– *two* poets of *extraordinary* parts.)

With hours and days trudging past,
my fantasies proved my best fun:
catalogues of errors and brain damage,
death, and needles in the bum.

With hours to kill, I examined
the Victorian Bridges's bearded face,
the old photos of Great Ormond Street
and his London Caledonian base.

But most, what caught my attention
was the panel furthest to the right:
acknowledgements to venerable bodies
who'd brought this history to light.

There was the borough of Islington
who donated biographical news,
and the various hospitals thanked
for their 19th century views.

Lying there, wincing from sutures,
my body collapsed, a right mess,
one name in particular stood out:
Oxford University Press.

I'd run through the worst countless times,
practised well how I would expire
to make them feel good and sorry
for having me callously fired.

I'd entertained all the options
which keep hypochondriacs amused,
then realised it's worst scenarios
which keep coffin-chasers enthused.

Are you sick, feeling down, Literati?
Are you feeling kind of dead or depressed?
Well you're assured of a publishing run
with Oxford University Press.

Haven't you heard it's the fashion
to decline the hale and hearty,
snub the living and only invite
the dead to the scholarly party.

Celebrate the germs and the scalpels
for they will be making your name.
The sicker you feel the more brightly
will shine that celestial fame.

Hurrah for dead, dying poets,
sick of consumption or gassed!
Murdered and cold in their grave,
at least they've an *interesting* past.

So here's a frank, open address
made from a hospital bed;
I'd rather be living unpublished
than be published by you and be dead.

LETTERS

OUP REVISITED
Dear Editor

May a lone (Oxfordian) voice make the tentative suggestion that the demise of Oxford Poets might do a little to lessen the current polarisations under such banners as "respectable", "Northern", "Southern", "an Oxford academic" (in reviewing Clare Pollard), and so on?

Or will it worsen the pigeon-holing by removing one of the holes? No doubt we shall watch with interest where the "Oxford" denizens end up, and wonder whether the backlists will be be up for grabs.
Yours sincerely
ERIC SMITH
South Warnborough

Dear Editor,

In the debate over OUP's ditching of their poetry list I've yet to see any reference to the *quality*, i.e. transcendent significance and beauty, of what we're losing by their decision, not even from the editor who selected these collections from the hundreds in circulation and passing through her hands. And not in Stephen Romer's Open Letter ('Open Letter To the Oxford University Delegates to Oxford University Press', *PR* Vol 88 No 4, p.102) either. Like many others, he referred to the poetry "renaissance" solely as witnessed by media coverage of the Laureateship and of schemes for promoting poetry in odd venues, like the Zoo or supermarkets. How these initiatives relate to the *qualities* of poetry isn't clear, but presumably they relate to possible sales and therefore profits, a response in the same domain as OUP's apparently commercial decision. As a non-poet but lover of poetry I find very little to distinguish much of the material in the OUP list and other grand lists from the thousands of poems one hears at readings or reads in small books or from competition winners – overwhelmingly random, variously sensitive, quirky, witty, original observations on the present quotidian printed in peculiar formats.
MATTHEW CLARENDON
London

20S A–Z
Dear Peter,

Can Neil Powell actually *read*? On p.3 of *The Radical Twenties* I say that my book is about England and English writers. He complains that there's no discussion of Scott Fitzgerald. On p.4 I explain why I shan't be saying much about "canonical" writers, including Virginia Woolf. Powell complains that I don't say much about Virginia Woolf. Oh, yes, he accounts for this by suggesting she's too upper crust for my taste, from which I infer he hasn't read the page upon page I devote to the at least as upper crust Nancy Cunard, Henry Green and Sylvia Townsend Warner. He attributes to me remarks which are clearly indicated as quotations, is critical of me for being critical of Betjeman for choosing to behave unpleasantly to his in-laws (Powell implies that there was no choice in it: Betjeman, being a gent was doomed to suffer from halitosis and an odd line in neckwear), and, as he claims that I mis-read *Howard's End,* which apparently opposes suburbia, must think that the Westminster Bridge Road and Liverpool Street, which draw Forster's ire, lie somewhere west of Metroland. To help him there, I recommend a London A-Z. For the rest, I fear he may be beyond help.
JOHN LUCAS
Beeston

FROM THE OCCUPATION
Dear Peter Forbes

In her sensitive review of Lotte Kramer's *Selected and New Poems 1980-1997* (*PR* Vol 88 No 4, p.28), Gillian Allnutt says that she doesn't know when Lotte Kramer began writing – the earliest work in the selection being published in 1980. I have admired Lotte Kramer's work for many years, and can tell you that she was published in small magazines at least as far back as 1971. I was involved with the Poetry One group at the time (based in South East Essex) and Lotte Kramer's poems frequently appeared in the group's anthologies, *Poetry One/Two,* and later *Assegai.* Two such poems were 'A Crucifixion' and 'Siege' (*Poetry One,* 1971). Her work also appeared in the Arts Council Anthologies, such as the piercing 'Dialogue' in the 1977 volume.

Further on in the review, Gillian Allnutt asks "How can I commend line-breaks when the poem deals with the loss of hardly less than everything?" I do not think that this is a rhetorical question here because it goes to the very heart of poetry/art and each practitioner must answer it for her/himself: How to use form to control content that threatens to overwhelm? I was reminded immediately of a very early poem by Sidney Keyes on the death of his grandfather, 'Elegy': "I am ashamed to take delight in these rhymes / Without grief..."

Just before the review of Lotte Kramer's volume there is an article by another poet who, as a child refugee, came to England without her parents, Gerda Mayer. Two of *her* poems appeared in the Arts Council Anthology of 1975: 'Salutation to Karl Marx' and 'The Civilised Muse'. How moving these testimonies are and how valuable the poetry that has come out of the scarred and blackened history of the twentieth century. Despite all the hype, the millennium should at least give us time to reflect.

It seems to be a period for considering the German occupation of so much of Europe. I have just read *To Siberia*, an immensely powerful novel by Per Petterson about two children – a brother and a sister – caught up in the occupation of Denmark, rendered into a spare and haunting English by the poet/critic/translator Anne Born. I commend it to all readers of *Poetry Review*.

Yours sincerely,

ALEX SMITH

Saffron Walden

FOR AND AGAINST HOLLAND

Dear Peter

I am sorry that Phil Simmons (Vol 88, No 4, p.11) misrepresents my argument about Jane Holland (Vol 88, No 3, p.86).

I did not say that Jane should be more encouraging of new poets just because she is herself newly published. New critics are entitled to their opinions. And new poets do not require special treatment. It is, of course, always easy to defend an ungenerous and unhelpful review as critical "rigour" (though it is striking that this kind of "rigour" is exercised rather more often on first collections than on the Selected Poems of heavyweight prize-winners). And I might have wished that someone who has just been helped up the ladder might want to give a hand to those on the rungs below instead of kicking them in the face because the ladder is too crowded.

My objection, however, was simply to the idea of the reviewer as game-keeper or nightclub bouncer which Jane's review exemplified ("there are too many people out there writing poetry") and which Phil Simmons seems to endorse when he talks of unhappy editors drowning in "oceans of substandard verbiage". Is it really true, as Phil

suggests, that "most serious poets" secretly share this view of their neighbours in the Republic of Letters? I thought we were supposed to be enjoying the revived popularity of poetry just now. If this is ever to be something more than a marketing gimmick, it surely means welcoming the fact that a great many people who used to write only in secret, are now prepared to send out their work for publication.

Thanks to the Poetry Society, and to the work of poets up and down the country working in schools and in their local communities, all kinds of people hitherto excluded from poetry now believe that poetry belongs to them too, not just to the talented, the educated, the lucky, the published and the successful. No doubt some of the poetry coming out of primary schools, adult education classes and community centres is what Phil would call "ill-thought-out and unoriginal". Perhaps some of it is limited by education, opportunity and technique. But it deserves to be taken seriously, and handled with the same care, encouragement and respect as the poetry that is published in, say, *Poetry Review*. You can't have one without the other. You certainly can't complain that there are too many people "out there" writing poetry and then expect anyone to want to read or buy it. If there are oceans of the stuff out there, these are only the oceans in which even the biggest fish must swim.

ANDY CROFT

Middlesborough

SOME CONTRIBUTORS

Robert Adamson was born in 1943. He has published seven collections, including *Waving to Hart Crane* which won the Christopher Brennan Award in 1996. He directs the Paper Bark Press.

Louis Armand has published work in journals internationally, including *Sulfur*, *Heat*, *Tinfish*, and *Meanjin*. Currently he lives and works in the Czech Republic and is poetry editor of *The Prague Revue*. His most recent collection of poetry is *Anatomy Lessons* (New York: x-poezie, 1999).

Iain Bamforth's collections include *Open Workings* and *Sons and Pioneers* (both Carcanet).

Lisa Bellear is a poet, writer, visual artist, academic and social commentator. Her first collection, *Dreaming in Urban Areas* (University of Queensland Press) was published in 1996.

John Bennett was born in England and now lives in Australia. His first book *A Measure of Place* appeared in 1994.

Peter Boyle was born in Melbourne in 1951. He went to Sydney University, where he was a contemporary of John Forbes. He has published two collections: *Coming Home from the World* (1996) and *The Blue Cloud of Crying* (1997).

Alison Croggon has published two award-winning collections of poetry, *This is the Stone* (Penguin Books 1991) and *The Blue Gate* (Black Pepper 1997). She has also written a novel, *Navigation*, and her theatre pieces have been performed around Australia.

M. T. C. Cronin was born in new South Wales. She has published three collections and in 1997 was awarded the Gwen Harwood Memorial Prize.

Diane Fahey was born in Melbourne. She has published six collections and her work is known internationally

Katherine Gallagher is an Australian poet and translator living in London. Her collection *Fish-rings on Water* (1989) and her translation of Jean-Jacques Celly's poems, *The Sleepwalker with Eyes of Clay* (1994) were published by Forest Books.

Peter Goldsworthy's *Selected Poems* appeared in 1991 and a new collection, *If, Then* in 1996. His five novels have been translated into many European and Asian languages; *Maestro* was published by Bloomsbury in 1991. He is working on a libretto for Australian Opera to be performed in the year 2000.

Paul Groves' latest collection is *Menage à Trois* (Seren).

Kevin Hart's most recent collection of poetry is *Wicked Heat* (Paperbark Press, 1999). An expanded *Selected Poems* is forthcoming from Bloodaxe Books. He is Professor of English and Comparative Literature at Monash University.

Dennis Haskell lives in Perth, Western Australia where he co-edits the literary magazine, *Westerly*, and works at The University of Western Australia.

Brian Henry is an American poet and critic who has lived and worked in Australia. He is an editor of *Verse* magazine.

Dorothy Hewett was born in 1923 in Perth, Western Australia. A prolific author of poetry, fiction, plays and non-fiction, her *Selected Poems* is published in the UK by Bloodaxe and a novel, *Bobbin Up*, and autobiography, *Wild Card*, by Virago.

Coral Hull was born in Paddington, New South Wales, Australia in 1965. She is an animal rights advocate and the Director of Animal Watch Australia, an online publishers, directory and resource site on animal rights and vegetarian issues. Her work has been published extensively in literary magazines in the U.S.A., Canada, Australia and the United Kingdom.

Michael Hulse is a co-editor of *The New Poetry* (Bloodaxe, 1993) and co-Editor of *Stand*.

Jill Jones is a Sydney writer. Her third book, *The Book of Possibilities* (Hale and Iremonger, 1997), was shortlisted for the National Book Council Awards and the Adelaide Festival Awards.

S. K. Kelen has written and published much poetry for over a quarter of a century. His recent *Dragon Rising* is a chapbook published by Thé Giõi Publishers in Hanoi.

Frank Kermode has been Professor of Modern English Literature at University College, London, Professor of English Literature at Cambridge and Professor of Poetry at Harvard. His many books include *An Appetite for Poetry*, *The Uses of Error* and most recently *Not Entitled: A Memoir* (Harper Collins). He is writing a book on Shakespeare.

John Kinsella's most recent volumes of poetry are *Poems 1980-1994* and *The Hunt* (both Bloodaxe). He is a Fellow of Churchill College, Cambridge, editor of *Salt*, and co-editor of *Stand*. *The Hunt* won the Western Australia Premier's Award this year and *The Age* Poetry Book of the Year Award.

Anthony Lawrence lives in Hobart, Tasmania. He has published six books of poems and his first novel *The Missing* is due out with Picador late in 1999.

Kate Lilley teaches feminist poetics and literary history at the University of Sydney. Her poetry is represented in the *Bloodaxe Book of Modern Australian Poetry* and the *Penguin Book of Australian Women's Poetry*. Recent work appears in *Jacket*.

Gerald Mangan's cartoons appear in *The Sonnet History of Modern Poetry* (Peterloo).

Lorraine Marwood's work has appeared as part of the Five Island Press's New Poets series.

David McCooey teaches at Deakin University. He has published poetry in many literary journals and is the author of *Artful Histories: Modern Australian Auutobiography* (CUP, 1996).

Lyn McCredden teaches literary studies at Deakin University, Melbourne. She is the author of two critical texts, *James McCauley* (OUP, 1992) and, with Rose Lucas, of *Bridgings: Readings in Australian Women's Poetry* (OUP, 1996).

Ian McMillan's latest collection is *I Found this Shirt* (Carcanet).

Rod Mengham lectures in the faculty of English at Cambridge University, where he is also a Director of Studies in English at Jesus College. His critical books include: *The Descent of Language: Writing in Praise of Babel* (Bloomsbury, 1993) and *Charles Dickens* (Northcote House, forthcoming 1999). He is editor of the Equipage series of poetry pamphlets and his own poems have been published under the title *Unsung: New and Selected Poems* (Folio/Salt, 1996).

Peter Minter's second book of poems, *Empty Texas*, is due for publication in 1999 with Paper Bark Press/Craftsman House. He is a contributing editor to *Boxkite*, and with Michael Brennan is editing *Terra Nova*, an anthology of new and innovative Australian poets.

Leith Morton was born in Sydney 1951. He is the author of three books of poetry: *Tales from East of the River* (Melbourne: Rigmarole Books, 1982); *The Fox* (Tokyo and Flagstaff: Kumon and Northland Books, 1990-2); *The Flower*

Ornament (Sydney: Island Press, 1993) and two volumes of Japanese translations.

Les Murray was born in 1938 in Bunyah, New South Wales, where he still lives. His work is published by Carcanet, including *Collected Poems* and *Subhuman Redneck Poems*, which won the T. S. Eliot Prize.

Sean O'Brien's latest books are *The Deregulated Muse* (essays) (Bloodaxe) and the anthology, *The Firebox* (Picador).

Glen Phillips is Associate Professor of English at Edith Cowan University In Western Australia. Apart from four volumes of poetry, his work has appeared in journals and anthologies in Australia, Asia and the USA. His *New and Selected Poems 1968-1998* is currently in press.

Peter Porter was born in Brisbane in 1929. He was educated there and Toowoomba during the Second World War and moved to London in 1951. He has been a freelance writer and broadcaster since 1968. He revisits Australia frequently and is the editor of *The Oxford Book of Modern Australian Verse*.

Ron Pretty has been writing and publishing poetry for nearly thirty years. His most recent book was *Halfway to Eden* (Hale & Iremonger, 1997). He edits the literary/arts magazine *Scarp* and is principal in Five Islands Press.

Judith Rodriguez has had nine books published, several of which won national prizes. *New and Selected Poems* and *The Cold* are still in print. She heads the Writing department at Deakin University and edited the Penguin Australia poetry series, 1989-1997.

Gig Ryan lives in Melbourne where she is poetry editor of *The Age*. She sings with the band Disband and has published six collections.

Tracy Ryan was born in urban Western Australia but now lives in Cambridge,England. She has published three books of poetry and a novel in Australia, as well as a short experimental work, *Slant*, in Britain. *The Willing* Eye (poems) will be out with Bloodaxe in July 1999.

Philip Salom won the 1987 Commonwealth Poetry Prize in London for best overall collection and toured the UK that same year. He has since published several collections of poetry – the most recent being his *New and Selected Poems* – and a prize-winning novel.

William Scammell reviews poetry for the *Independent on Sunday*; his latest collection is *All Set to Fall Off the Edge of the World* (Flambard).

Tom Shapcott has published 6 novels and 14 volumes of poetry. He received the Struga Gold Wreath Award in 1989. He is currently Professor of Creative Writing at Adelaide University.

George Szirtes' *Selected Poems* are published by OUP.

Andrew Taylor is the author of eleven books of poetry. He teaches at the University of Adelaide.

John Tranter spent his youth on a farm on the South-east coast of Australia, attended country schools, and took his BA in 1970. Thirteen collections of his verse have been published. In 1992 he edited (with Philip Mead) the *Bloodaxe Book of Modern Australian Poetry*. He is the editor of the free Internet magazine *Jacket*, at http://www.jacket.zip.com.au

Chris Wallace-Crabbe was born in Melbourne in 1934. He has published many books with Oxford University Press.

David Wheatley is an editor of *Metre*. His first collection, *Thirst* (Gallery) was shortlisted for the Forward Prize.

John Whitworth's collection *The Sonnet History of Modern Poetry* is published by Peterloo.
